CLOTHES
ON AND OFF THE STAGE

TWO SILHOUETTES

A. Ann Harding as Bianca in "The Taming of the Shrew."
B. John Drew as Petruchio.

CLOTHES
ON AND OFF THE STAGE

A History of Dress
From the Earliest Times
To the Present Day

BY

HELENA CHALMERS
AUTHOR OF "THE ART OF MAKE-UP"

Illustrated by the Author

. . . Our actors are very sensible that a well-dressed play has often brought them as full audiences as a well-written one.

ADDISON, in *The Spectator*

NEW YORK : LONDON
D. APPLETON AND COMPANY
MCMXXVIII

Republished by Gale Research Company, Book Tower, 1976

**Library of Congress
Cataloging in Publication Data**

Chalmers, Helena.
    Clothes, on and off the stage.

    1. Costume--History. I. Title.
GT510.C5 1976   391'.009   73-180965
ISBN 0-8103-4033-X

FOREWORD

The aim of this volume is to present a history of costume in continuity so that data upon any period, together with established precedent in stage dressing, may be readily available when needed for theatrical production.

Supplementing extensive personal research in the art galleries and museums of Europe, the author has been a close student of such standard authorities as Planché, Fairholt, Vecellio, Shaw, Knight, Strutt, Hope, Flaxman, Herodotus, Hottenroth and the Münchener *Bilderbogen;* also of old manuscripts, effigies on monuments and in tombs, sculpture and wall paintings. Among various modern works those of Chamberlain, Gosse, Fraser, Read and Wornum have each proved helpful in the assembling of the great mass of facts needed for a reference book of this kind.

H. C.

CONTENTS

CONTENTS

ILLUSTRATIONS

ix

ILLUSTRATIONS xiii

CLOTHES
ON AND OFF THE STAGE

CLOTHES ON AND OFF THE STAGE

CHAPTER I

PRACTICAL HINTS ON DRESSING FOR THE STAGE

N the everyday business of dressing most of us give some thought to the suitability of color and form while selecting clothes for the especial hour and its engagements. Different costumes are intended for morning, afternoon, business, travel, sport, or evening wear. True, we behold the order not always observed, but no sane woman would play golf or go on a shopping tour in a dinner gown. The introduction of the ensemble idea has proved a godsend to many who seem born without a sense for color grouping and the appropriate. By reducing the number in a costume to one or two, a woman of poor taste has no excuse to go wrong in choosing hats, stockings, shoes, handbags, handkerchiefs, gloves, jewelry—even the inevitable flower is to be had in harmonizing shades; capable saleswomen may advise those who need a guiding hand.

Every one has enough sense of color value to realize that while sky-blue, pink and the like are appropriate for festive events, they are not the correct hues for a funeral. In real life we do not purposely don bright colors for solemn events. Nevertheless, not being able to foresee exigencies, a woman may be dressed in a costume rivaling the plumage of the flamingo or the peacock for brilliance and yet have to face the most tragic, the most heart-rending experience of her whole life. Hilarity is not unknown among those who, following an ancient custom, go robed in black for a certain period out of respect for the dead. Herein lies the chief difference between dressing for the stage or off.

The most important requirement in a theatrical costume is that it should provide an index to the part portrayed, and this is accomplished by considering the psychological effect of color upon an audience. Not only must those selected suit the part, but also the emotions to be emphasized in certain scenes of the play. The player knows ahead what is in store for the audience; the actress understands that it would take a rare artist indeed to wring tears from those in front if a flamingo-colored gown flashed before them; on the other hand, any director will object to dark colors in a comedy, black being considered absolutely deadly.

Another point that needs careful attention is the effect of artificial light on color. Material for stage use should always be selected by electric light with, if possible, colored bulbs placed in the sockets. With clear lighting, which is diffused through straw or lemon-colored gelatine screens, most colors hold their own; navy blue and dark green, however, appear as black. A suit of the former color, both youthful and cheerful in daylight, develops unexpected sobriety. Brown, which would be classed with these two for street use, becomes much lighter, the yellow in its composition warming up with the play of

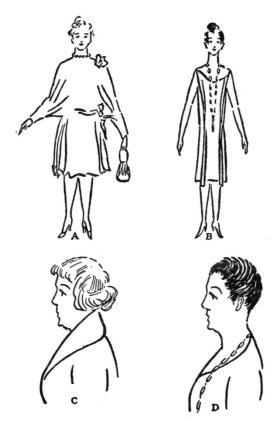

PLATE I. WHAT LINES CAN ACCOMPLISH

A. A girl inclined to be plump using lines in her costume which tend
to exaggerate; *i.e.*, wide sleeves, side pleatings on skirt, girdle knotted
on hips, flower on shoulder, large choker necklace and width in hair
dressing.

B. A girl emphasizing her height and slenderness by the use of
vertical lines.

C. A fat woman accentuating her size by badly arranged hair and a
collar which thickens her throat and humps her shoulders.

D. A woman of the same build with hair carried up from the
ears and rolled on the head; the flat neckline and long necklace also
tend to slenderize.

light. Brown and tan suits are for comedy. Blue is
ever tricky; some light shades look gray.

With deep ambers, light yellow is turned to white,
orchid frequently to gray, while jade becomes often a
dull blue, especially if the material be crêpe. Taffeta
retains color more successfully. This material, together
with satin and any other that reflects light, will always
appear brighter; for this reason a black velvet gown is
always darker than one of black satin.

When it is the business of the player to choose his own
colors and costumes, care should be taken to attain har-
mony and at the same time supply contrast. It is an old
law of the theatre that the leading lady has first choice
of color. If you are a beginner, defer not only to her
but to the other women of the cast. For many productions the costumes are designed and made under the
supervision of some especial director, the player merely
going for fittings. A dress rehearsal means just that—
all clothes must be ready and worn as though for the first
performance. The director then passes on every detail,
ordering such changes as he deems necessary.

The costume as far as possible must be cut on lines
best suited to the player's figure, which will be silhouetted
against the back drop with every curve and every angle
in bold relief. A very tall, thin girl should endeavor to
widen and shorten hers. All vertical lines in trimming
will tend to increase its length, while horizontal effects,
like the hoops on a barrel, will broaden and shorten. The
wide sleeve so fashionable at present, especially if of a
brighter color than the center of the gown, will carry the
eye across the figure and accentuate its width; a gaily

colored girdle or narrow belt of a different shade from the gown will give the same result.

The short, plump woman, if her line of business requires height, should avoid these things. A belt will cut her figure in two, besides broadening it. If a gown is of two colors, the brighter should always run up and down through its center, and the sleeves be kept dark and, if possible, tight. Darker shades in stockings will give the leg a slimmer outline. High heels will do their bit if the fastening on the shoe is considered Cross strappings which broaden and shorten the foot should be avoided by short, fat women who usually have broad feet, wide heels and large calves. If the shoe is made with an ankle-strap, a lengthwise band like that on the old Egyptian and Grecian sandal should run up the instep from the toe piece, thus narrowing the foot. Bobbed hair should rise in a wave on top and be kept flat at the sides. A pompadour on a man adds greatly to his height. For contrast, part the hair in the middle and plaster it down; almost two inches will apparently disappear.

Clothes must be theatrically effective. Fine stitches, exquisite needlework, tiny French eyelets and the like are thrown away on garments intended for use in the theatre. Basting is imperceptible but, as it is not desirable to drop flounces, sleeves and other parts of the costume while on the stage, strong stitching is advisable. Two or three large hooks and eyes should be placed where most needed, speed and security being indispensable. It may be necessary to dress quickly before a performance; time is always limited between the acts, and all actors are possessed of a mad desire to get out of the theatre as quickly as possible afterward.

A contrast of color such as a vivid lining in a cloak or hanging sleeves has theatrical value. Feather fans and brilliant beads are effective. Jade, fuchsia, tangerine, rose, violet, etc., are all telling shades. Fine beads, and those that catch light are always preferable to the dull variety, are lost unless the gown affords a background of a deeper or lighter shade, or is of another color. Jet is invaluable for the stage; so are sequins. Directors have admired spangled tunics, which are purchasable in all department stores, ready made, while in their eyes expensive but not striking dresses sometimes pass unnoticed.

White chalk beads, if sewn on black materials in clusters representing bunches of grapes or flowers, appear as white muslin cut out and appliquéd. The same beads on white resemble machine-made embroidery. One of the most remarkable "flops" in costume was an imported gown fashioned of steel beads sewn in solid formation to bands which hung from the neckline to the hem around the entire dress; from the auditorium these looked as though made of gray ribbon.

Real lace requires a background—black on white or colors, and the reverse. By playing violet lights beneath lace skirts, the pattern was shown up in the ballet "Laceland," a number in a past edition of the "Follies."

Some dresses of fine material fail utterly, while one bought for twenty dollars may look like a gown costing two hundred. The stuff must drape easily, be of a certain richness of color, or catch light.

For the many materials mentioned in this history, certain modern substitutes may be used, and to offset expense the amateur, by using dyes and colored lights, can achieve some stunning results with unbleached muslin—which, however, must be dipped in a cotton dye before a basic, or aniline dye, procurable in exquisite shades, can be used. Obtain some cotton and aniline dyes and, by following directions as to the materials best suited to each, experiment by varying the quantities of water and dye; one color may be applied over another after the first has dried; irregularity in the dipping also gives good results.

In the decoration and accessories of the costume, the psychological effect on the audience must again be considered. Frivolous trimming such as ruffles and flying ribbons create a light, happy mood, whereas swinging earrings, bobbing curls and waving plumes may keep an audience from sobbing when sadness is the effect aimed at. The bold, bad lady of the play can be subtle; she need not be loaded with birds of paradise, gorgeous brocades and blazing jewels.

The actress who is to wear a train should rehearse in this until she becomes accustomed to it and free from the necessity of kicking it aside, or awkwardly stepping on it. If the actual gown intended for the performance is used, the train should be protected from dirt during rehearsal by stitching muslin around the bottom, both inside and out, to a depth of two or three feet. An actor should practice handling a drape. There is a trick of sitting down when wearing a bustle or a hoop skirt; the former should be pushed sideways by a movement of the body, but, it goes without saying, never by the hands; the latter must be given a slight upward lift at the back to prevent the entire front from rising. In a tearful part an actress should be provided with a handkerchief to dry her eyes and nose, unless, of course, where the character is of a certain type, an apron, shawl or sleeve is used. There are many little things that go to make stage style. An actress not only considers her dress, but also what she wears under it. This need be very little, but it must be smooth; no fancy lace ruffles, no ribbon loops or silk flowers should adorn it, as these cause lumps and shadows to appear on the gown. Underwear should never be suggested; above all, it must never show. Even a shoulder strap will do it. In fact, there is no practical reason at all for the shoulder strap. At a recent amateur affair one of the performers unknowingly presented a dowdy appearance by permitting the audience to glimpse, through the black chiffon yoke of her dinner gown, variously colored shoulder straps belonging to several totally unneeded "undies"; furthermore, the lace-edged, pink ribbon-run slip climbed a diagonal path from her right armpit to her left shoulder.

For a slight girl, a brassière firmly supporting, but not flattening the bust may be worn accompanied by bloomers, and the latter should, preferably, be of the gown's color; a slip may also be worn if the dress is transparent or fashioned of a material which clings when walking. A slip will also be found necessary if, in the course of a play, the actress stands in an open doorway up stage with strong "spots" playing on an outdoor scene beyond. The slip, again, should match the gown in color and be so adjusted that it does not reach the bottom of the skirt's hem. If the gown is of georgette or other thin material, it must extend below the top of this hem, otherwise an inch or so of transparent shadow will play there and through it garters and legs will be visible. Once a slip is properly hung, anchor it with a pin before it shifts and shows below the skirt. Petticoats are never worn except in plays of a rural type, which call for starched calico dresses. They should be secured by large safety pins, not draw strings. Dropping a petticoat on the stage is embarrassing, to say the least. Never wear a white petticoat with a dark skirt, for it will show when seated.

Supplementing a brassière, women who are in the slightest degree fleshy should wear a hip corset; one that pushes up in front, causing a bulge or bad break in the costume, must be avoided.

All garters should be as inconspicuous as possible. Never let loops of ribbon and flowers hang from a round one. A garter rolled above the knee is likely to cause a bulge in the gown when seated. The exhibition of hosiery these days, particularly free to the public gaze when the wearer is ascending stairs, is too often an affront to the fastidious eye; seams winding diagonally about the leg suggest nothing so much as the stripes on a barber's pole. For the stage, the seam must run exactly in the back of the leg, or a bow-legged effect will be produced. Clocks should be vertical. Not a wrinkle must be left about the ankle, for the tiniest fold will take shadow from the strong lights and create an impression of slovenliness, or of a thin ankle in a loose fitting stocking. And this rule applies to the entire costume. Wrinkles or bulges caused by undergarments catch definite shadows and also give the idea of a poor fit. Draw the stocking up tightly and secure it; men should do the same with socks. Tights must never show the slightest wrinkle. If possible, wear suspenders, gathering any looseness about the straps above the buttons and securing with safety pins. Silk stockings should not be worn if the character is one who, logically, could not afford them. If the person portrayed is in mourning and black stockings are demanded, those of the chiffon variety should not be selected because, when worn on the stage, the skin is certain to show through and produce anything but a somber effect.

Stockings and shoes must harmonize, or afford contrast, both being chosen with due consideration for the colors of the gown.

Long vamps on shoes are ugly, while short ones tend to diminish the length of the foot. Be careful in the arrangement of colored leathers. Light shades stand out and, unless well placed, may widen or foreshorten the foot in an ugly manner. The tall, small-boned girl with a long narrow foot running in A widths, can use cross-strappings and wide-color designs with perfect confidence. Large calves do not accompany slim feet, therefore she may indulge in stockings of the lightest shades.

Many beginners are under the impression that their feet will be inconspicuous on the stage; on the contrary, there is no place in the world where they are more in evidence. Men should always see that their shoes are freshly polished; before leaving the dressing room flip a cloth about them, as powder may have settled on the shine.

When playing a gentleman, be very careful about all the little niceties of dress. The coat should lie smooth against the collar; the sleeves must allow a glimpse of linen; but then, again, the wrists will have an awkward appearance if the sleeves are too short; and the legs, too, if the trousers are worn the least bit too high. When wearing a vest, be sure that the audience does not get occasional glimpses of a belt. See that every detail of costume is correct for the time of day, and for the suit worn. Do everything to convey the impression of being well groomed.

A woman's skirt should hang well and never be shorter in front than behind. Particular attention should be paid to the neckline. If the material is allowed to bulge across the chest, dark shadows will appear, causing the neck to look thin. Have the front edge absolutely flat against the skin from shoulder to shoulder. All costumes of opaque materials made with set-in sleeves should be provided with dress shields, for patent lotions cannot be relied upon. When the play calls for the wearing of a nightgown, tight, flesh-colored trunks, such as are used by dancers, are worn with a smooth gauze vest over them. Nothing like underclothes must break the lines of the body.

When a young girl is attempting to play a middle-aged or elderly woman, a large-sized corselet with a layer or so of wadding sewn to its entire inner surface will enlarge the figure and yet permit the gown to fit without grotesque lumping.

For an extremely old woman a shawl can be pulled up in folds about the shoulders and back of the neck, thus creating a humped appearance. Padding can be stitched in a high-necked waist to form a rounded back.

When playing in gowns of the seventies, eighties and nineties, the figures of most girls of to-day do not look well without a high, boned corset. The waist must be small and the basque should fit without a wrinkle. As these corsets are very hard to find, a fitted underbodice, heavily boned, will help—provided the figure is first laced about the waist line by modern stays as high as can be obtained.

Picture hats should be tilted on the side that will be most shown to the audience. The small, tight hats often throw the eyes into shadow. Everything possible should be done to avoid this. On the stage, a hat can be worn a little farther back on the head and at an angle which, if attempted on the street, would be ridiculous.

In choosing colors, an actress should not "kill" ner own. Pastel shades are always pleasing and should be used by blondes, whose delicate tinting must never be lost. Brunettes may indulge in the vivid hues without fear, always provided that these do not clash with others on the stage.

Red, the color of fire and heat, should not be worn by a red-headed girl, whose glorious locks radiate warmth. She will look better in blue, a cold and, therefore, neutralizing color, if her eyes match. Green is more effective with brown, or greenish eyes.

All blue-eyed women with white skins look well in blue or green, but those of dark or sallow complexions should avoid these colors; they will find both trying, and the green will often prove disastrous. However, as all eyes appear dark at a short distance from the stage, this advice is not of superlative theatrical value.

A costume, with all its accessories, should be rehearsed in, so that no difficulty will later be encountered in sitting, walking or gesturing. On the first night it must be put out of mind, for all illusion will inevitably be lost if the audience senses that an actress is conscious of her clothes. If every detail has been considered, and the whole judged by some competent person, she may rest assured of being a picture at all moments.

An actress, as a rule, innately carries this idea into private life, always appearing with her hair in place and her clothes in good taste for the occasion, for she realizes that a dowdy, careless appearance will not win her advancement. Competition is very strong, and charm in her ensemble may attract the attention of agent, author, director, or manager, with a resultant engagement. The good word may even be passed along as in the old song about "a friend of an intimate friend of an intimate friend of Frohman's."

CHAPTER II

SILHOUETTES AND HIGH SPOTS

S we look back over the long procession of body coverings used in all ages, our attention is arrested here and there by some, at the time, new and striking form. Every period of the world's history has a certain style of dress, either all its own or borrowed from some previous fashion. It may be unique and notable and used but once. It is frequently transitional. Again, it may be climactic. Something originates in a modest way and, being seized upon by the dandies, the sirens or the mob, develops into huge proportions like an inflated balloon, doomed to ultimate collapse and obliteration, or shrinkage to a tiny souvenir of a gorgeous past. Because the idea is simply exhausted, or, occasionally, as a reaction of war, what follows is a plain or sober fashion, the very simplicity of which takes the world by storm.

This constant change of fashion has created a procession of silhouettes, a glimpse at any one of which should indicate some particular period. While to most of us the form may be familiar, we do not know to wha: exact date it properly belongs. Any one who aspires to be a director in the theatre, however, should be well informed on such a point. At the dress rehearsals of a costume play he should know, the instant an actor steps out on the stage, whether his silhouette is correct, for there the glaring faults will appear. Mistakes in detail can be adjusted on close scrutiny.

Costumers are not infallible; running short of what is absolutely correct, they may substitute a style unheard of until perhaps fifty years after the period of the play. An Empire coat with three or four little shoulder capes is most certainly out of place in the play of "Little Women," the first act of which is dated 1863, yet a New York costumer took a chance on director, actors and public not knowing any better. Often, gowns of 1840 are made to take the place of those of 1860; and the eighteenth-century coat is subjected to much fanciful handling.

In the study of costuming, consider history, for the two walk hand in hand. Famous rulers have done much to influence fashion; the whims of kings, queens, famous beaux and belles, actresses and courtesans, have had more to do with changes in the mode than all of the tailors and modistes.

A Spanish princess has a goiter on her neck; to cover it she wears a little ruffle about her throat—and lo! the ruff. A French coquette is thrown from her horse and her hair falls down; she ties it up with the aid of her garter—and all the world of women is soon wearing a huge headdress called the Fontange, after the beauty with her first-aid garter. We can no more separate clothes from history than salt from seasoning.

Reviewing the subject in detail, its most arresting forms —or may we call them high spots?—seem to have been as follows:

Tunics, dating from the very Dark Ages.

Togas, mantles of magnificent proportions and class distinction.

Cross-garterings of leather thongs, rope, straw or golden cords.

Trousers, from the curious open-work, pajama-like affairs which Paris is portrayed in on Mount Ida, the Oriental suggestion of those worn by the Amazons, and the baggy, ruffled "bracæ" of the Gauls, through their various disguises to the snugly fitting trousers of Beau Brummel, slashed over the instep, later fastened under it, and of various degrees of fullness, the greatest amplitude being manifested in those known as Oxford Bags, a reversion to the loose ones of the Gauls.

Tights, trunk-hose, bombasted breeches, petticoat breeches and the skin-tight black satin breeches of George III, to don which men were obliged to climb upon something and then step down.

Wimples, covering all of the hair, to which were added gorgets, concealing all of the throat.

Chin-bands, the best invention for routing double-chins ever known.

Cases, contrivances placed on the end of the natural braid and linking strands of false hair, which fell to the ladies' knees or farther, according to their pleasure.

Enormous headdresses of the fifteenth century, known as horned, hearts, steeples and hennins.

Ruffs, at their largest in 1582, when the term "cart-wheels," as applied, was descriptively appropriate.

Cracowes, wooden soles with raised portions under the ball of the foot and the heel, and a projecting point designed to support the extremely long toe of the shoe (these were later forbidden by proclamation, as traffic, even in those days, presented problems).

Chopines, shoes with cork soles varying from three to

eighteen inches in height, a fashion of Constantinople copied by the ladies of Venice.

Chaperons and roundlets, headdresses and hats respectively, evolved from the hood with its hanging liripipe.

Surcoats and their offspring, the cote-hardie, a dainty jacket ermined and jeweled.

Houppelandes, long, all-enveloping garments with wide sleeves, gaily foliated.

Drapes, those one-arm holed wraps of the Middle Ages used by all Romeos.

Lacing, introduced on the outside of the gown in the eleventh century, transferred in the sixteenth to instruments of torture called busks, that reduced the waist, by overlapping the ribs, to thirteen inches.

Age of draperies, when, in the twelfth century, men and women loaded themselves down with voluminous apparel of all kinds.

Parti-colored age, so named because a vagary of fashion decreed that costumes should have a sharply marked color line through the center, thus one leg might be red and the other black.

Heraldic age, when the coat of arms of the wearer was emblazoned on the surcoats worn over armor (shown with stunning effect in a recent production of "Henry IV," by the Players' Club).

Age of satin and ribbons, lasting through the period of the Stuarts and immortalized in Sir Peter Lely's portraits of the court beauties, veritable poems in satin, hanging in Hampton Court Palace.

Dagged fashion, with the edges of garments cut out to represent leaves.

Cauls, open networks of gold wire, pearls, or jewels

forming caps, which have cropped up in all ages and are especially endeared to us as the most favored head-covering of all Juliets.

Farthingales, huge wheels of bone suspended about the hips, in the latter part of the sixteenth century, and over which the stomacher gown was hung, combining to create one of the ugliest costumes of all time.

Panniers, broad and tilting, providing a resting place for Madame's elbows.

Hoop skirts, wide spreading, tipping, requiring an expert touch in the act of sitting to prevent their rising in a scandalous arch.

Simarres, graceful Florentine gowns.

Milan bonnets, jauntily perched and gaily feathered, inseparable from any visualization of Henry VIII.

Doublets, originally practical jackets of two thicknesses, doomed to much slashing and even bombasting to the weight of five pounds, when, as the "pease-cod-bellied," they were worn by the laced dandies of 1583.

Virago sleeves, large open ones of the sixteenth century.

Engageants, those frivolous lace ruffles hanging flirtatiously from the elbow of the eighteenth-century sleeve.

Solitaires, black ribbons laid in gracefully negligent fashion around the necks of gentlemen at the court of Louis XV.

Watteau or sack-back dresses, immortalized in the eighteenth century by Watteau and numerous court painters.

Fontanges, absurd headdresses of tower-like proportions which necessitated lowering the head when passing through a door.

Cavalier costumes, the most debonair of all time for men.

Coats, long, short, side-pleated, buckram skirted, laced, cuffed, uncuffed, cutaway and "swallow-tailed."

Cocked hats, whose tilt had a language all their own.

Periwigs, achieving distinction when they imitated the luxuriant locks of the Grand Monarque, later taking on every conceivable size and form.

Empire gowns, their grace of line a flashback to the ancient Greek.

Stocks, bandages for the throat resembling surgical dressing, worn by gentlemen during the early nineteenth century.

Leg-o'-mutton sleeves, atrocious affairs of 1830.

Pantalettes, little modesty pieces for feminine ankles in the bashful forties.

Poke bonnets, charming frames for pretty faces.

High hats, the most pompous and dignified of all headgear.

Chignons or "waterfalls," which cascaded from the crown of women's heads in the justly ridiculed seventies.

Bustles, hideous, fashionable and considered modest by some in the seventies and eighties.

Large sleeves of the nineties, immortalized by Charles Dana Gibson in his cartoon of the suddenly surprised couple on the sofa, when the girl's sleeve is flattened on the side nearest her beau.

Trains, graceful through all the ages, ever suggestive of the regal, and in the early twentieth century worn on all street dresses.

Pompadours, named for the Marquise de Pompadour

and revived by the Gibson girls and their mothers early in this century.

Merry Widow hats, cocked on the pompadour and loaded with plumes.

Hobble skirts, freakish, dangerous and but a passing fad in 1910.

Slit skirts, sensational but sensible, since they made walking possible in garments measuring less than a yard around at the bottom.

Rainy day skirts, sponsored by a woman's club and predecessors of the "trotteur" and the knee-length skirt of to-day.

Bobs and short skirts, making the present one of the most remarkable and revolutionary periods in the history of fashion.

CHAPTER III

THE OLD STONE, NEW STONE AND METAL AGES

HE people of northern countries were obliged to wear the skins of wild animals for body covering, as weaving and spinning were unknown arts. The inhabitants of warmer climates utilized dried grass in the making of kilts; strung necklaces of teeth, stones, etc., about the shoulders, and adorned themselves with crudely wrought armlets and anklets. Even a clumsy, bulky piece of fur can be artistically draped; doubtless the flapper of the Old Stone Age wore hers with a certain chic and knew the latest edict of fashion as to length.

Leather thongs were used to hold the fur in place. As all early people were obliged to spend much time in hunting and fighting, freedom of the body was arbitrary; therefore, all barbaric races left the right arm and shoulder unhampered by clothing.

The earliest foot-covering was a piece of fur, roughly gathered about the ankle by means of a leather thong.

Scrapers for preparing skins, large bone needles, hollowed stones, evidently used as mortars for grinding colors with which to paint the body, flints, spears, heavy clubs, slings and bags of leather containing stones, have been found in ancient caves.

All barbarians are fond of personal ornamentation; besides rough jewelry in its usual forms, the ears and under lip were probably decorated with teeth and bits of bone in a manner identical with that practiced by savages of to-day, to whom, undoubtedly, this fad of the caveman has descended.

Movie comedies picturing the prehistoric man are familiar; Larry Semon, Buster Keaton and others have been seen in the costume just described, while Leon Errol and Harry Kelly were sartorially correct in their caveman sketch in "The Century Girl," save for the comic anachronism of Kelly's high hat.

Relics of the New Stone Age are found on all continents, among them being the spindle-whorl, which proves that the arts of spinning and weaving were known. Crude garments of wool and flax were worn in Europe, and very likely cotton fabrics in India, all local products.

The Metal Age, during which copper, bronze and iron came into use, began nearly four thousand years before Christ. Improvement in materials and ornamentation followed.

CHAPTER IV

THE EGYPTIANS AND THE ARABS

The Egyptians

THEIR history has been recorded from 4000 B.C. The Pharaohs, or rulers, reigned until the conquest by Alexander the Great, 332 B.C. During this period the costuming was purely Egyptian. For authority we go to the wall paintings, bas-reliefs, statues and treasures of the tombs. There were thirty-one dynasties: during the fourth, 2900-2750 B.C., the pyramids were built; in the eighteenth, 1580-1350 B.C., were erected the obelisks now seen at New York, London and Rome; in the nineteenth dynasty, 1350-1205 B.C., the great Rameses reigned, and the children of Israel were oppressed. Herodotus, the Greek historian, visited Egypt in the fifth century before Christ and wrote of its costumes and people.

The opera of "Aïda" is costumed in the period of the Pharaohs.

From 332 B.C. the Ptolemies (Greeks) ruled until the death of Mark Antony in 30 B.C. Historians tell us that Egyptian sculpture came under the influence of the Greeks, who introduced their gods and their arts into Egypt. Charles Knight says: "It is uncertain how much, or if any part, of the costume of the Pharaohs was retained by the Ptolemies"; however, there is a sculpture in the great temple of Dendera, Upper Egypt, representing Cleopatra and her son, Cæsarion, dressed in the costume of the Pharaohs. This is usually worn by actresses when playing the Queen. Sarah Bernhardt wore a mixture of ancient Egyptian, Greek and Arab, her hair a glorious red in striking contrast to Jane Cowl's black bob. Cleopatra was thirty-nine when she died, and granting that age could not wither her, the lady was hardly a flapper—a fact which actresses should consider when essaying the rôle.

From 30 B.C., the Roman emperors held sway until the successful invasion by the Arabs, 638 A.D. The opera "Thaïs" is timed during the early Christian period, when Egypt was under Roman rule.

From very early times Egypt was famous for its linen, so sheer that often tunics fashioned of it were worn one over another, arranged in starched folds resembling modern accordion pleating, an effect plainly visible in many statues. Priests were allowed to wear linen only in the temples, in such regard was the fabric held; all mummies were wrapped in sheets of it.

The wall paintings in the British Museum give evidence of the Egyptians' skill as dyers, a profuse intermixture of colors revealing a predominance of crimson and yellow.

The Kilt.—The principal garment of the men was made either of plain linen or some richer material, with a heavily embroidered girdle, often decorated with jewels, placed over it. To the kilt of a Pharaoh was added a lion's tail.

The Tunic.—Of sheer linen descending to the feet, this garment was worn sometimes over, sometimes under, the kilt, with long winglike sleeves. An old wall painting dated four thousand years before Christ, shows an Egyptian princess strolling in a tight-fitting garment like the

PLATE II. EGYPTIANS, TURKS AND HINDUS
A and B. Egyptian king and queen.
C. Egyptian woman of the better class.
D and E. Turkish women.
F and G. A rajah and a Hindu woman wearing a sari.

dress slip of a modern woman, save that it is cut more immodestly low in the neck and more modestly long in the skirt, reaching to her ankles, the whole suspended by straps over the shoulders. Later, a broad girdle encircling the hips, was drawn very tight with long ends descending to the feet. Fringe was used as border trimming.

Jewelry and Ornamentation.—The upper part of the body was frequently covered with wide necklaces and breastplates of gold, rich with lapis lazuli, red jasper, turquoise, gold beads, and enameled work in which the Egyptians excelled. The Louvre and the British Museum are well stocked with jewelry taken from the tombs; scarab rings, bracelets and armlets in the form of serpents, pearl earrings, large pins to stick in the hair, wonderful beads in blue and green, rings in profusion—for all classes wore them—also amulets, placed in the tomb at time of death, to ward off evil.

A very pretty decoration for women was the laying of a blue lotus flower on the head so that it hung over the center of the brow. One wall painting shows a gathering of women—possibly an afternoon tea or the first federation of women's clubs—each adorned with a lotus flower in this fashion. These ladies were not strangers to cosmetics, their complexions showing a much fairer coloring than that of the men; apparently some form of liquid whitening was in use. Their eyes, as well as those of the men, were blackened with kohl, a powder considered beneficial to those organs. From the quantities of porphyry jars we know the women were much addicted to perfumes and ointments. The hands and feet of both sexes were stained with henna.

Footgear.—The sandal had a long curved-back toe

piece woven of palm leaves. Embroidered leather shoes, heelless and soft, were also in use.

Hairdressing.—Wigs of black wool were much worn by both men and women, and, as usual when wigs are in vogue, the natural hair was either cut short or shaved. Herodotus says the priests had shaven heads, whereas in other countries they left their hair long. The Horus lock was a braid hanging over one ear, a decoration of royal males in childhood. The beards of mummies are often woven with gold thread. False ones representing braided hair extending down from the chin, appear on coffin lids; one made of lapis lazuli inlaid on a gold base is on the recently discovered case of Tut-ankh-amen. The beard was only allowed to grow from the tip of the chin, but to the length of six or seven inches. On the stage, unless care is taken to stiffen, the beard waves in the air, every time an actor speaks, in a ludicrous way suggesting a goat's.

Crowns.—The uræus was a serpent of gold wound about the head, its use restricted to royal personages. It frequently is incorrectly placed on the headdress of dancers and actresses impersonating Egyptians, no matter of what rank or character. A royal diadem of 3000 B.C. belonging to Tut-ankh-amen is of gold made in a simple fillet style. A vulture and a serpent (uræus) surmounting the band are removable. Carnelians, lapis lazuli and turquoise beads stud the fillet, also the long bow ends at the back. Gold uræi decorated in the same manner hang each side of the bow. The double crown of Egypt was a combination of the ancient white crown of Upper, with the red one of Lower, Egypt.

THE ARABS

In 638 A.D. the Arabs conquered Egypt, northern Africa, Spain, and were proceeding to overrun France when checked at Tours by the Franks in 732 A.D. They remained in Spain for eight hundred years, influencing costume and leaving the tourist marvelous bits of architecture to revel in. Their ever picturesque costume is seen in Egypt, Algeria and Morocco to-day and has furnished the modern movie hero with an opportunity to drape himself gracefully in the burnous.

Historians inform us that there are two races of Arabs, those who derive their descent from the primitive inhabitants of Arabia, and those who call Ishmael their ancestor. The Ishmaelites wandered in the desert, having neither cities, houses nor fixed habitation, and dwelling only in tents; the Bedouins of to-day are their descendants. They are migratory and often robbers. Each tribe is headed by a sheik.

The Cachi.—This was a small felt hat, brown, red or white with a silk tassel of another color. Several are worn one over the other—on occasions of ceremony to the number of fifteen—but no matter how many, the red always on top. In one scene in "The Son of the Sheik" Valentino appeared in a cachi, the tassel of which was so long it hung over his shoulder like a curl.

The Haik.—An oblong piece of white wool or cotton cloth from two to three yards long and often striped, laid over the head and held on by agals (rings) made of camel's or goat's hair pressed tightly down about the brow. In the photoplay just mentioned Valentino, while he is being dressed, impatiently gives these rings an extra push down on his head. The haik falls in folds each side of the face, in a sandstorm one end being caught across the nose and mouth.

The Burnous.—A cloak of very generous proportions is made with a large hood and worn over the haik, the two fronts either joined by a band about five inches wide across the top of the chest or tied with tassels. In the former case the garment is put on by thrusting the head up through it. Tassels are sometimes used as decoration about the hem. A Moor of high degree in Tangier wore a burnous of rose-colored cashmere heavily embroidered in gold; on one of his long tapering fingers glowed a great ruby. He was bearded as are nearly all Arabs. In northern Africa one has constantly the feeling of living in Biblical days, owing to this combination of beard, haik and burnous.

A sheik sometimes wears a short, tight-fitting coat embroidered in gold and tasseled; under it a white vest shows, opening in a deep V, a style common to Turkey and Arabia. A belt of bright colored, striped silk is wound about the waist and knotted on the left hip. Baggy trousers reaching to the knees are met by stockings or high leather boots. Sandals, when worn, have high leather side pieces. An elaborate leather belt is placed over the silk sash with the pistol holster directly on front of the figure.

In "The Sheik," the bandit wore a huge hat resembling an overturned plate, entirely covered by waving plumes.

The Boor'cko'.—The face veil of the woman, a piece of linen or black muslin almost the length of the body, is suspended from a band about the forehead by means of a vertical strip placed over the nose; the two outer edges are caught back to the band, leaving the eyes visible. With the boor'cko' is worn a large hooded cloak enveloping the entire figure. Arab women of social standing are not seen much on the streets. Very poor women run about bare-legged to the knees, while the rest of the body is swathed in what looks like a white sheet (not a clean one) held carefully across the nose in such a way that one eye peers at the tourist.

Silks, of exquisite colors interwoven with gold thread, are used for more elaborate clothes. Brilliant squares or oblong pieces, often gaily striped, are fastened to the head, shoulder or hip; trousers of silk or cotton, long tunics, red shoes turned up at the toes, and large circular earrings complete the costume.

CHAPTER V

OTHER ANCIENT NATIONS

THE BABYLONIANS, ASSYRIANS AND CHALDEANS

HEIR history begins several centuries later than that of the Egyptians. The writings of Herodotus and the tablets found in excavations of ancient cities tell of their culture and learning. They believed in spirits and were astrologists, the Chaldeans being famous for their powers to foretell events by the stars.

Assyrian bas-reliefs show that strong, brilliant color was used in costume, vermilion predominating. The Babylonians dressed their idols in blue and purple. Linen was more common than wool.

The Tunic and Mantle.—Both were long, fringe being used a great deal for borders; sleeves, elbow length. The round neck, also the edges of sleeves and skirt, received much decoration in the form of embroidery. An outer tunic or peplum was so folded about the hips that the trimming with which it was bordered ran diagonally, one row above another from skirt hem to waist, causing the costume to be drawn in about the knees and hips. The fringed mantle was folded with the upper part over the lower, then placed under the right arm and fastened on the left shoulder, thus creating more diagonal lines.

Hairdressing.—The hair was arranged in a series of

corkscrew curls. A curling iron was undoubtedly applied to the beards, which were long, square cut and presented alternate rows of spiral curls and a circular, roselike formation.

A high, round bonnet rising in tiers, sandals strapped to the bare feet and jewelry in the form of heavy armlets and bracelets completed the costume.

Nineveh fell in 606 B.C., Babylon in 538 B.C.

THE MEDES

After the fall of Nineveh, the Medes reigned.

The Tunic.—The Medes wore long, full-sleeved tunics, raised in front and drawn through cord loops placed at each side of the waistline.

The Mantle.—Its fullness also was caught up through rope girdles in front, thus binding and distorting the figure.

Hairdressing.—Hair was curled like that of the Assyrians; the women's heads roped with pearls. Round bonnets were worn.

THE PERSIANS

In 558 B.C., Cyrus overthrew the Medes and built up the great Persian Empire, which lasted until 330 B.C. The bas-reliefs from Perseopolis, and the famous Frieze of the Archers done in colored tiles found in the Palace of Darius at Susa, give us a procession of quaint figures from which the main points about the Persian costume may be easily gathered.

The Tunic.—The Persian tunic was long, with a sleeve spreading in fanlike pleats from the elbow. The dress was invariably pulled in tight about the hips, ending in

PLATE III. ORIENTALS
A and B. A Mede and an Assyrian king.
C, D and E. Jews of Bible days.
F and G. Chinese lady and gentleman.
H and I. Japanese gentleman and lady.

elaborate and heavy draperies. Borders were much used.

The Mantle.—A cloak, through which the head passed, was worn looped up over the sword hilt.

The Bonnet.—Tall, curiously wide at the top, the bonnet rather resembled a fez worn upside down. The tiaris was a cap or bonnet, covering both ears and tied down under the chin. The hats of the workmen were conical.

Long hair and beards were arranged in precise curls.

Shoes were pointed.

The Persian king is represented walking under a parasol carried by an attendant. The tunics of the workmen are short, with elbow length sleeves over vests which show the V opening at the neck.

Wool and silk were popular materials.

THE PHŒNICIANS

They antedated the Jews in Canaan, a country lying along the eastern shore of the Mediterranean, and were noted for textile fabrics, embroideries and purple dyes, the last obtained from the murex, a shellfish found on the Phœnician coast and which is said to have yielded the famous Tyrian purple.

Besides inventing the art of phonetic spelling, the Phœnicians were great mariners and largely responsible for distributing universally the products of different countries, such as silk, wool, linen and cotton, thus being an important factor in the history of clothes.

THE JEWS OF BIBLE DAYS

The Tunic.—The Jews wore long, tight-fitting tunics with armholes or wide sleeves (made in one piece without seams, according to Josephus), having a large opening at the neck extending from breast to back. For the rich, tunics were of handsome materials, the borders bound in bright contrasting colors; also of linen, always a notable fabric among the Israelites. Cotton and wool mixed were used by the poor.

The Mantle.—The outer garment consisted of a piece of square cloth, voluminous enough to permit of wrapping about the body. In very ancient times a fold could be pulled over the head for protection.

Turbans were adopted later in imitation of the head covering so popular throughout the East.

Sandals were worn.

Women.—Their dress was colorful and as rich in decoration as its wearer could afford. The women of the household spun and wove the materials used for the family wardrobe. Embroidery was much used as ornamentation; clothes dyed blue, purple and scarlet are frequently mentioned in the Bible.

The Hair.—The Jews shaved their heads and beards in time of mourning, repentance or distress and in certain ceremonies of purification. At other times long, flowing beards were considered not only beautiful but dignified. Taking a man's beard in your hand and kissing it was an intimate act signifying love or the utmost respect. In great grief the beard was torn or neglected, while being deprived of it by force stood for degradation and servility. For many references to the beard, see the Bible.

Fragrant ointments were applied to the hair of the men; women braided, perfumed and decorated theirs. The tires alluded to by Ezekiel are thought by some to be ornaments for the hair, crescent in form; others hold that the tires mentioned in Judges and by Isaiah were used

to adorn the neck.   There would seem to be good reason
for this last opinion, as necklaces of crescent-shaped pen-
dants are common among Oriental people to this day.
These tires were worn not only by men and women but
also hung about the necks of camels.

Bracelets and armlets, usually large and often of great
value, were very popular with both sexes.

CHAPTER VI

THE CHINESE

HE Chinese, inhabitants of that vague land called "far Cathay," invented satin, velvet, brocade and silk of a peculiarly soft texture. Embroidery unsurpassed and of brilliant hues, was worked in prehistoric times. The discovery of the secret of silk making by Europeans is attributed to the return of two Greek priests from a pilgrimage to China, with the eggs of the silkworm hidden in their staves. The Ming Dynasty, famous for the glaze and decoration of its pottery, lasted from 1368 to 1644 A.D.

Very few historical facts are known previous to the eighth century B.C. Confucius, the great teacher, lived from 551 to 478 B.C., and the Chinese wall was begun in 221 B.C. for protection against the Huns. Ancient armor was of strong rawhide.

The Dress.—Old prints show us that the cut has altered but little. In order to prevent discomfort to the body, loose garments of light silks, gauzes and linen, the sleeves wide and hanging free of the wrist, are used in summer by the wealthy; loose cotton trousers, with an overhanging shirt and a widespreading bamboo hat—sometimes cut to the hat and trousers—constitute the peasant's costume. A raincoat made of reeds is used in stormy weather. Such cloaks are common to peasants in many countries. In winter. long robes of silk and crêpe, with jackets and mantles of fur, protect the well to do, while the poor construct body covering from the skins of the rat, mouse, squirrel, etc.

"Sam" is the Chinese word for a short jacket; a "chang sam" is a long one. A narrow collar band of silk, or of fur in winter, finishes the neck. "Min" means top and "di" under, either being used in conjunction with "sam."

"Fo" are trousers; both the trousers and the jacket are sometimes lined, which gives us "kak fo" and "kak sam."

A tight jacket worn under the outer one in winter is called a "gun sun," and a vest used for the same purpose, a "bon sum."

"Quan" is a skirt and is used in conjunction with "di" and "min."

A full dress jacket for men is the "mar quar."

"Mo" means a hat for a man or a child. "Di mo," a large hat; "si mo," a small one. There are innumerable hat and hood styles for children, all showing a desire to entertain the juvenile mind; for instance, one suggests a lion, another a dragon with embroidered eyes; a variety known as the "mon yi mo" or pussy hat, is a caped hood with cat's ears placed each side of the head. This same idea was used in England in the Middle Ages. A style for women originating in Soo Chow, a city near Shanghai, is called the "Soo Ban"; this is a bandeau for the head called elsewhere a "ban ton."

The official full dress of a man, a gown of much dignity, is the "po," while "lung po" means the dragon's gown, the costume used on state occasions by an emperor.

Trousers.—Female servants wear them always; their mistresses sometimes appear so clad about the house but skirts are considered correct for more formal wear. Even the men do not think trousers gentlemanly unless camouflaged by a long gown over which a jacket is sometimes placed.

Rules for the Cut.—The jackets and trousers can be of the same cut for both sexes, the difference being that those of the women are always trimmed, even if of self material, but the men's never. The ordinary male jacket is usually fastened down the right side by means of loops caught over gilt buttons; if in mourning, the latter are of crystal. The "min sam" or top jacket, however, buttons down the front. This would be considered most immodest for a woman; hers must always close on the side, the only exception being an intimate affair worn next to the body. All children wear trousers and jackets.

The clothes are made without pockets; a Chinaman sticks a fan at the back of his neck, and stuffs other necessaries in his stockings, which are woven of cotton or silk.

Footgear.—Shoes are "hai" and boots "her"; when of a high cut they become "her-hai." Cloth, satin and velvet are used in their making and the felt soles, several inches thick and heelless, are finished with a strip of leather placed across the bottom. Shoes are whitened, not blacked. The Chinaman makes himself comfortable with slippers, stockings or naked feet on entering his home.

Hairdressing and Ornamentation.—The Chinaman has not been compelled by law to wear a queue since 1912. The fashion was imposed by the conquering Manchus about three hundred years ago. Two-thirds of the queue was made up of false hair, braided in. Silken cords were used in the same way. The women often place an ornament over the right ear. In Manchuria the headdresses are large and elaborate, with massed flowers and pendant pearls. Conspicuous on the modern stage are the tiaras of Jeritza in "Turandot," and Florence Reed in "The Shanghai Gesture."

Lily Feet.—In the old days all Chinese women were supposed to be frail, delicate and languid. Big feet were considered very clumsy and unladylike. Hence the fashion of binding the feet of children to arrest their growth. The smaller the lady's feet, the greater her beauty. The deformed bones she hobbled on were known as "lily feet." With the advent of athletics, they have gone out of style. The foot of a servant was never bound; in fact, some Chinamen had several ornamental consorts boasting lily feet, but secured one useful wife with undwarfed number sixes to attend to his comfort.

The Wedding Ceremony.—Red has always been the Chinese color for happiness; a bride wears a red "hong sam" with a veil of the same hue, which is lifted from her face after the ceremony by the groom; when queues were the mode, this gentleman had his braided with red cord. The bridal gown is always elaborate; a headdress has pearls hanging across the face and is of a beautiful, intricate design. The "hand quan," or skirt, is hung with bells, and a broad collar covers the shoulders.

Jewelry.—Agate and jade (the latter known as "yu") are much used on buckles, clasps and other forms of jewelry. The Chinese have always excelled as gold and silversmiths.

The first act of "East Is West" takes place on one of the so-called "flower boats," on which the professional singing girls of China, who are hired by the owners, entertain the rich men who make the boats a rendezvous. These women are dressed in gay colors, with elaborately deco-

rated hair. During the play, the Chinese idea of what
constitutes modesty is well depicted. Ming Toy, when
alone on the scene, unfastens her jacket at the neck to ape
American girls dancing in a cabaret, but is overcome with
confusion when surprised in the act.

CHAPTER VII

THE JAPANESE

EUDALISM held sway for centuries in Japan; not until the great revolution of 1869 was it swept away. A few years before, an expedition from the United States, headed by Commodore Perry, had been successful in opening to foreigners the hitherto closed port. About 1872 the progressive young Mikado insisted on breaking through the old rule which forbade any one to look upon his face. In 1885 we find him not only appearing in European dress but ordering his court to do likewise. Many people became alarmed at the rapidity with which the Japs adopted up-to-date fashions, fearing the unique beauty of their national costume would be lost. These Orientals persisted, however, in spite of general protest, even giving up the elaborately dressed and oiled coiffures and submitting to the modern bob. The latter is not unbecoming but French clothes seem peculiarly out of place.

With the adoption of European ideas, women stopped shaving the eyebrows, plucking out the eyelashes and blackening the teeth after marriage, evidently concluding that the old feudal idea of a wife making herself so ugly that no one would seek her out as a recipient of illicit love was, after all, a poor way of retaining the admiration of a perfectly good husband.

WOMEN

A widow signified her intention of remaining faithful to her departed lord and master—until she changed her mind—by shaving her head and tying her obi in front.

The Slip.—Of wool, cotton crêpe or silk, this garment is worn as underwear by the un-Europeanized Japanese woman, the border showing where the kimona laps from the left side over on the right in front. It is colored scarlet for girls, white and sometimes purple for married women.

The Kimona.—Two or three are placed one over another, their edges showing about the neck. In bad or very cold weather, extra ones are added for protection. The peculiar pigeon-toed gait of a Japanese woman is attributed to the closely clinging kimonos constantly pulling the right foot inward.

The sacred geishas of the temples wear twelve, but only of two colors, red and white. The robes of the dancing geisha girls are covered with gay embroidered flowers and, with the obi, are of gorgeous materials. The hair is elaborately dressed and ornamented; on the feet are white "tabi" and sandals of black lacquer, and a fan waves in each hand.

The Obi.—A sash over three yards long by twelve inches wide is wound two or three times about the figure well above the natural waist line and tied in a bow at the back. A silk band three or four inches wide (or a gold buckle) keeps the bow from shifting. For a married woman, or one of "a certain age," the bow presents a square appearance; flappers tie them at a coquettish slant. The brilliant colors of the obi vie with those of the kimona, and rich materials such as gold brocade, etc., make this article of attire often very expensive.

Hairdressing.—Before bobbing and simple European styles were copied, the coiffures were marvelous to behold, so intricate that, once up, several days passed before the hair was touched again. The tiny wooden pillow of the Japanese, together with the quantities of coconut oil used in the dressing, helped to make this possible. The hair was twisted and rolled over wire shapes, oil applied to create luster, and ornamental pins called "kanzashis," representing brilliant flowers, were stuck in it; quite a shower of them pointing in all directions.

Footgear.—White "tabi" (socks), worn by girls and women, which come up over the ankle where they fasten with hooks, are fashioned with the big toe having a pocket to itself, like that of a thumb in a mitten. The slit thus created between the large toe and the others is used to hold the cord or thong by which the "zori" (sandals) are fastened to the foot. Above the "tabi," snugly fitted, are worn white silk gaiters.

MEN

The natives go barefoot, wear "zori" (see women) or the wooden clogs called "geta." The latter are three inches high and are attached to the foot through the slit in the "tabi." Sandals are removed before entering a house, as no shoe of any kind is worn when indoors by either men or women.

Dress.—Owing to the excessive heat at some seasons, the un-Europeanized native is apt to go half naked; in the rural districts, totally so. Even the jinrikisha men, when

Japan was first opened to travelers, ran about the city streets wearing little more than "birthday suits."

The popular jacket and trousers of cotton crêpe, either blue or white with colored borders, combined with straw sandals and a "kasa" (a mushroom-shaped hat of split bamboo or straw held from the head by wires to permit ventilation), make up a popular dress for many men. The Japs have a raincoat made of fine matting; in the country, rough affairs like those of the Chinese resemble thatched straw roofs.

Japanese letter-carriers were tattooed in brilliant colors over the entire body; the actual costume consisted of a scarf knotted about the brows to catch perspiration, a loin cloth and straw sandals. The Japanese pilgrim is dressed all in white with a huge straw mushroom hat, sandals and a staff. A matting raincoat tied across his shoulders serves as his bed. Shinto priests wear their clerical robes only when at service in the temple, in contrast to the Buddhist who walks robed in rich mantles.

The Hair.—Most Japs show crops of bristling black hair, the result of periodically shaving the head in childhood. Before the advent of a European haircut, the front part of the scalp was shaved after a boy reached the age of fourteen. The long back locks were then coiled in a knot. The hair of little girls was allowed to grow after they were five years old, save for a round spot as big as a silver dollar, which was kept close shaven on top of the head. Bangs were much affected by Japanese children.

CHAPTER VIII

THE HINDUS

HE date of the Aryan invasion is about 1500 B.C. A subsequent mixture of races caused the establishment of four hereditary classes, eventually developing a system of castes with laws prohibiting any intermingling. Marriage, breaking bread together or indulging in any form of personal contact was forbidden. These sharply drawn lines showed in the costume, creating great diversity of form.

Materials.—The manufacture of cotton originated in India. It is believed to have been worn there as early as linen was in Egypt. Delicate muslins and calicoes of Indian manufacture, both plain and figured, were carried to Persia, Arabia and Egypt before the Christian era began. The fineness of these products was such that pieces of considerable width could be drawn through finger rings. The Hindus were famous also for the manufacture of silks of extraordinarily fine texture. The goats and sheep of Cashmere and Tibet furnished the wool for the India shawls so fashionable in early Victorian days.

The Costume.—The large class of Hindus known as snake charmers, also the coolies and the Bhils, are scantily clad, but always turbaned. Many castes wear cotton drawers, turbans and shawls; others, long or knee-length robes over trousers, and still others go bare-legged. Sashes, shawls, and the ever popular turban, of which there is an infinite variety in size and form, complete the costume.

The clothes of the rajahs are made from the richest materials known. Plumed turbans are strung with pearls and decked with rare gems; the tunic usually tight fitting and belted has a shoulder piece like a cape running down in points to the waistline, heavily decorated with fringe and ropes of pearls.

The Sari.—The most important item of a woman's dress is a voluminous veil or wrap of muslin, gauze, or silk worn around the waist with one end falling to the feet, the other crossed over bosom, shoulder and head. The right hand and shoulder are, as a rule, visible. Under it is worn a tunic, with either long or short sleeves, reaching to the feet. Drawers frequently show below the tunic or sari, held to the leg by anklets. Rings in the left nostril, with sometimes a pendant jewel; bracelets, necklaces and headdresses consisting of square plaques from which chains of pearls are suspended each side of the face; a fan, shaped like a battle-axe, of plaited woven straw—all these are part of the costume.

CHAPTER IX

THE GREEKS

HE Greeks first appear in history in the eighth century B.C.; the legendary date for the Trojan War is 1194-1184 B.C.

The Elgin marbles in the British Museum, the collection of Grecian vases made by Hope and the writings of Homer, are the standard authorities for the costume of the Greeks in the heroic age.

On the frieze of the Parthenon the following articles of men's attire and weapons are found: a short tunic; the chlamys, a knee-length military cloak fastened by a clasp on the right shoulder (this one appears on the statue of the Apollo Belvedere); a broad-brimmed hat known as the petasus, or Thessalonian, and a close skull cap of leather; a buskin, a high shoe reaching well up the calf, known later as the cothurnus; a large circular shield; a sword which hung horizontally under the left armpit; a helmet topped by a crest; a cuirass; bows of goat's horns with arrowheads attached to feathered shafts; quivers lined with skins; spears with heads shaped like leaves; others with a head made of three crescents, evidently intended for hunting. Various portions of the female dress can be seen on the statues of Thalia, Ceres and Diana: a long tunic, the upper arm covered by catching the material together at regular intervals with buttons, as on the statue of Thalia; the peplum, an oblong cloth hanging or wrapped about the bosom; a girdle, holding the tunic below the bust; sandals.

The vases show the Amazons in clothes suggestive of the Orient: trousers; embroidered tunics with long set-in sleeves; the chlamys; the Phrygian cap, always made with the soft peak turned forward. They carried a small shield like a half moon known as the pelta. Furs also appeared. In later years the inhabitants of Thrace were clothed largely in furs brought from Russia.

Homer gives detailed descriptions of the arms carried by Achilles, Agamemnon, Ajax and the rest of the warriors. They were made of various metals such as gold, brass, tin and steel, the shields being decorated with dragons, Gorgon's heads, etc. Achilles must have been a resplendent figure in a corselet of gold with a helmet covered with gilded horsehair. Homer says the skins of animals were hung over the cuirass. This armor should always be placed over a short tunic. Greaves (leg armor) were fastened to the naked flesh, with the feet sandaled or bare.

The costumes of Troilus (who was the son of Priam) and Cressida are of the heroic age. The Greeks in "A Midsummer Night's Dream" are sometimes Elizabethan.

Materials and Ornamentation.—Wool and flax were most in use. Herodotus describes Arabian sheep; from them was procured the Milesian wool, considered by the Greeks the finest of all. Later on flax was mixed with silk. Clothes made of pure silk were very costly, as this material was brought from the East. Homer speaks of elaborate embroidery as not uncommon; a diplax (double mantle) belonging to Helen of Troy, portrayed the battles of the Greeks and Trojans. Aristotle speaks of the magnificent pallium of purple embroidered to represent cities, gods and men, which was made for Alcisthenes, 520 B.C.

Homer describes the armilla or bracelet of a Grecian woman as like a "twisted spiral."

THE AGE OF PERICLES

This was the period when Greece was at the zenith of her glory; art flourished and magnificence prevailed. From 470-431 B.C. the plays of Æschylus, Sophocles and Euripides were given in the theatre of Dionysus at Athens. The costumes followed the usual lines, but were elaborately and richly decorated. "Timon of Athens" is dated a little later during the time of Alcibiades.

The Tunic (also called the Chiton).—This principal garment was always worn next to the skin. To its crinkled, clinging folds we owe much of the beauty of Grecian statuary. For stage use, two large squares of cheesecloth or *crêpe de Chine,* closed by seams on the sides to within twelve inches of the open top, wet, wrung out and left tightly rolled until dry will, when the body is wriggled through, give a good imitation of the impression one receives from the marbles. Such a costume can only be worn three or four times without rewetting. (It should always be kept rolled when not in use.) When worn by women, fibulæ or buttons held the loose edges of the tunic together over the upper arm, while the fullness was confined about the waist and under the bust by cords passed around the waist, over the shoulder, between the breasts, about the waist again—this time a little lower—then knotted. The folds of the material should be coaxed to fall gracefully by gently pulling the goods up between the

PLATE IV. ANCIENT HEADDRESSES

A. The Phrygian cap as worn by Paris on Mount Ida (from the Hope Collection).

B. The petasus or Thessalonian cap.

C. The pileus, the conical cap of a Roman workman, covered by a fold of the toga (detail of a wall painting at Pompeii).

D. A Persian dress showing the fanlike sleeve.

E. The Assyrian bonnet.

F. The Persian bonnet.

cords. The tunic should always reach the floor The tragic actresses of the Comédie Française, so used to donning these costumes, walk with a long, pushing glide which prevents tripping on the hem.

The Dorian tunic of the men was a short woolen one fastened by large clasps on the shoulders. One side was left open to insure greater freedom in athletic exercises. Spartan women are supposed to have worn it also. The Ionian tunic was long and ample, with wide elbow sleeves.

The Strophion.—A forerunner of the corset worn by women consisted of three bands; the lowest confined the hips, the highest passed under and supported the bust, while the remaining one defined the normal waist line.

The Super-Tunic.—This reached to the waist and was worn for extra protection. Either the tunic was folded over on itself and allowed to hang loose, or a separate garment was cut in points at each side, which, when weighted with lead, caused the material to hang in zigzag folds that swayed with every movement of the body.

The Peplum.—An oblong piece of goods, about four yards long by two wide, formed a mantle worn by both men and women; the material passed twice around the body under the arms, was brought up over the shoulders and secured by closely winding it about the figure. For extra protection this wrap could be pulled over the head and was so adjusted in times of mourning.

The Peplos.—This was a veil of thin material large enough to envelop the entire figure when thrown over the head.

The Pallium.—An ample cloak worn by philosophers, as also was the tribon, a coarse black or brown mantle.

The Himation.—A cloak capacious enough to drape

about the body in folds. These mantles were all without fastening and required much skill in graceful draping.

The Chlamys.—This garment was a distinctly military cloak falling to the knees and fastened by a clasp on the right shoulder.

Footgear.—Sandals, worn chiefly by women, consisted of a thick leather sole with an ornamental piece on the instep, held by straps about the ankle. Another variety resembled the Japanese tabi, with a strap of leather separating the big toe from the others. The cothurnus or buskin was a laced shoe of ornamental leather reaching to the middle of the calf, sometimes lined with the skin of a small animal, the head or paws hanging out at the top. We of to-day might adopt this idea and vary the sameness of our goloshes. The buskin was used by actors when playing tragedy, its high raised sole making the player more conspicuous. Socks were worn by comedians. Hence the expression, "socks and buskin."

Materials.—Those most in use were of wool and flax. All the silk was brought from the Orient and therefore a luxury. Linen was imported from Egypt. Ornamentation took the form of borders and small or large patterns, repeated over the entire goods. Thus we find frets, such as the well-known "wall of Troy," edging the tunics while unrelated spots, stars and the like, covered the center space. Large designs, for example, birds embroidered in gold, silver and colored threads, appeared with striking effect. No cotton goods were used by the Greeks for clothing. Silk was manufactured after A.D. 551.

The Hair.—The men wore it curled across the forehead and falling in ringlets to the nape of the neck or shoulders. The busts of Sophocles, Pericles, Homer,

Diogenes, Epicurus, Demosthenes and many others represent them with beards. This fashion lasted until 336 B.C.
when Alexander the Great, so the story goes, commanded
the Greeks to be shaved, fearing that in the intimate warfare of those days the beards might be clutched by the
enemy. Every result attainable by the use of a curling
iron is to be found on the marbles. Beauty parlors were
not needed because everybody of any standing at all had
six slaves. All married women parted the hair in the
middle and wound it into a classic, or Psyche, knot at the
back of the head. A string drawn from the nose backward should run into the center of its base; from its ex-
tremity curls often dangled. A simpler form consisting
of a coil on the nape of the neck also is seen. Fillets and
ribbons bound the hair.

Only the courtesans affected mitres (this class also carried hand mirrors).

Jewelry and Ornamentation.—Earrings, necklaces,
bracelets, armlets and anklets were popular among women,
who also carried fans and parasols. The men wore finger
rings and carried walking sticks, but had no armlets or
anklets like the Romans. This difference frequently leads
to error in stage productions.

Respectable women rarely appeared in public, and then
always covered by the peplos. Like the Chinese, the
Greeks used flame-colored wedding veils held to the brow
by gold fillets in the open key design. A bride wore
rose color (again the Chinese color for joy) and a golden
girdle, on her face a patch of gold leaf. A ring was presented at betrothal, though it was not the custom to wear
a wedding ring.

Slaves.—Their hair was cropped close to the head. A

PLATE V. GREEKS AND ROMANS

A and C. Statues of Diana and Thalia; clothes of the heroic age.
B. Statue of Hadrian showing a lorica and paludamentum.
D and E. Athenians in the age of Pericles.
F and G. A Roman matron and the toga as worn by Edwin Forrest.

short tunic of rough material was worn under a leather coat called a diphthera, barefooted or sandaled.

The Dance.—The costume varied with the occasion; garlands and wreaths for festivals, white at funerals and full armor (the Greeks still wore the cuirass, crested helmet, and greaves of the heroic age) in the military dances. The Greeks were compelled to dance till the age of thirty.

The Mask.—As the actor had to appear in huge amphitheatres, it was necessary to make him as conspicuous as possible. Not only were the soles of his buskins thickened to increase his stature, but his garments were heavily padded and a large mask was set on his shoulders with features enlarged and vividly painted. Each mask was made to represent a certain character. A device was placed in the mouth opening by which the voice was projected to a great distance. What a relief it would be if some of our Broadway Thespians were so equipped!

CHAPTER X

THE ETRUSCANS AND THE ROMANS

The Etruscans

HE Etruscans flourished some centuries before the city of Rome was built, 752 B.C. The present section of Italy known as Tuscany corresponds to the ancient center of Etruscan territory. At one time Etruria meant all the land from the Tiber to the Arno. Excavations of the tombs have brought to light wonderful collections of vases made of red clay and coffin lids with figures in high relief, also many wall paintings.

From these we find that the principal articles of dress were the tunic and the toga, the latter wrapped with one shoulder left bare. Garlands of flowers were placed on the hair, which was short; the face was clean shaven. Gold was used in profusion. Besides bracelets in the form of serpents, very long earrings, rings, breast plates, fillets, clasps, and vases for perfume, all fashioned of solid gold, implements of warfare such as helmets, spears, lances, etc., made of the same precious metal, were apparently common.

The curule chair, also the patterns of many garments worn later by the Romans, were of Etruscan origin.

THE ROMANS

Antiquarians dispute various details, but the tunic and the toga are conceded to have been the chief articles of attire of the very ancient Romans.

The Fasces, Saga, Paludamentum, Trabea and Etruscan Togas.—The last king of Rome, Tarquinius Priscus, expelled in 509 B.C., introduced these from Etruria, also the custom of triumphing in a golden car drawn by four horses; he surrounded the axes borne before important public officials with bundles of elm or birch rods called "fasces." These symbols of power were tied with purple ribbon and represented the right to execute a death sentence; they were carried by the Roman lictors during the Republic which lasted from 509 to 367 B.C. Each consul was accompanied by twelve lictors dressed in white tunics with a cloak fastened on the right shoulder. This mantle was the Etruscan saga or paludamentum, a military cloak resembling the Grecian chlamys.

The shape of the trabea, also copied from a garment of that name worn in Etruria, is disputed. It is, however, conceded to have been a robe of white wool with scarlet stripes running horizontally, the whole edged with a purple hem or border, the latter not applied but made one with the garment; this, Cicero says, was "twice dyed." When knights in solemn procession wore the trabea, they were called the "Trabeati." According to Virgil and Livy, it was also used by kings and priests.

The togas known as picta, pura and prætexta and the tunica palmata, were Etruscan.

There was little change in fashion before the days of the Empire. Coriolanus is supposed to have died in 490

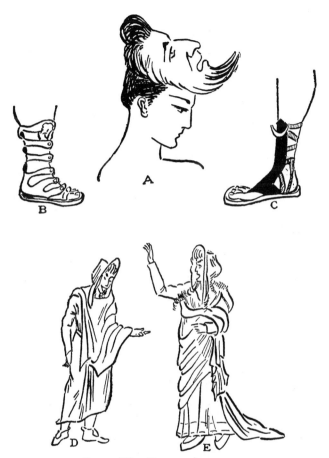

PLATE VI. ROMAN ACCESSORIES

A. A Roman actor with mask pushed up listening to the director
(from a Pompeiian mosaic).

B. Shoe worn by Edwin Forrest as Spartacus.

C. The "calceus lunatus" worn by John Philip Kemble as Cato.

D and E. Two Roman actors wearing masks. One has shoes with
padded soles to increase his height (from a wall painting of Pompeii).

B.C., and Julius Cæsar was assassinated in 44 B.C., yet despite the interval of time, the costuming is the same for
both Shakespearean plays dealing with these characters.

THE EMPIRE

During the reign of the first emperor, Augustus Cæsar,
27 B.C. to 14 A.D., the Græco-Roman period was at its
height, influencing costume as it did art.

The Tunic.—The tunic was of wool, left in early times
in its natural yellowish tint. With men the length was a
matter of choice. Cicero says that Cataline's companions
had tunics reaching to their feet and he implies that they
were considered effeminate. The tunica palmata, worn
by generals when celebrating a victory, was covered by
palms embroidered in gold. The "laticlavian" tunic of the
Roman consuls is made for stage use with two bands of
purple encircling the neck opening and extending down
to the hem. It is stated by some authorities that a "clavus" was a round spot which dotted the tunic all over,
while other antiquarians contend it was in the form of a
purple band either sewn on or woven into the tunic. On
those of the senators and magistrates the band or "latus
clavus" was broad, while for knights the "augustus clavus" was narrow. No girdle was worn with this tunic.
In early times this seems to have been the general fashion,
but evidently it became bad form, as Cæsar was criticized
for the looseness of his clothes.

When two tunics were used, the one next the body,
called "subucula," served as an undershirt, of wool for
men, but almost invariably of linen for women.

The Greek fashion of catching the upper edges of the
tunic together over the upper arm with buttons, was copied

by Roman women. Sleeves were set in later, these gradually attaining great length.

The Fascia.—A woman's girdle encircled the body under the bust and about the waist and hips, its long knotted ends hanging to the floor in front of the body.

The Toga.—Over the tunic was worn a voluminous wrap in which the Roman was swathed when appearing in public. Like the Grecian cloaks, it had no fastening. Its exact form has been disputed, but for stage use all togas dating from the days of Talma have been cut after a pattern in use at the Théâtre Française. This is a semicircular form having the segment of a circle folded over on it. In the early Roman period the toga was made of wool left in its natural yellowish color. It was a garment of magnificent dimensions, being cut so that the length was three times that of its owner. This was necessary in order that the two ends of the semicircle's diameter with their leaden weights might just clear the floor before and behind the body when the garment was in place. To adjust, after the segment is folded back on the semicircle with the curved edges down, lay the goods over the left shoulder so that a weighted end nearly touches the floor in front of the left arm. Reach behind the figure, gather up all the fullness in folds, which must then be carried up under the right armpit across the chest, and flung over the left shoulder. If the garment is correctly cut the weighted end should fall to the ankle. By inserting the hand inside the material flung across the chest, a portion of the sinus (also called pectora, according to Ovid), *i.e.,* the folds first draped over the bosom from the left shoulder, can be pulled up, thus forming a pouch or pocket in which the Roman probably carried his sudarium (pocket handkerchief)

In later times the togas, like the tunics, were made of silk and other fine materials and received much decoration. The toga was never used in periods of mourning.

The toga prætexta, bordered with a band of purple, was worn by magistrates, censors, priests, and later by emperors; by freeborn boys until fourteen years old; by girls until marriage.

The toga virilis, also called pura and libera, was assumed by boys when they laid aside the prætexta. The right arm was kept within its folds during the first year as a mark of modesty.

The toga picta, purple, embroidered with golden stars and rich Phrygian needlework, was worn by victorious generals, also emperors, consuls and other high officials on great occasions.

The toga candida, rendered pure white by the application of chalk, was used by those aspiring to some public career. This was their only body covering; as much as possible the body was left exposed in order to display wounds contracted in the service of the country.

The toga sordida or pulla, colored brown or black, was for the lower classes and accused persons.

Among women the toga was worn only by freed slaves and prostitutes.

The Stola.—A long loose garment with a wide border distinguished women of honorable standing.

The Palla and the Pallium.—The palla, a voluminous unsewn wrap like the Greek himation, shared popularity with the pallium, a cloak of cloth with interwoven flowered designs and bordered with fringe. Both could be placed over the head, then wrapped about the body under and over the arms and shoulders. Horace says the palla was also worn by Roman tragedians.

Veils.—Veils were of various colors; like the Grecian, a bride's veil was red and called the flammeum.

The Lacerna.—A large piece of woolen cloth colored black or brown was worn by common people over the toga when traveling or in bad weather and fastened by a clasp on the right shoulder. Although despised by people of quality in early times, this garment was adopted later on by all classes. When red it was known as the birrhus. A hood (cucullus) was sometimes attached.

Footgear.—The mulleus reached to the middle of the leg, leaving much of the foot exposed as in a sandal. It was of red leather and originally the foot covering of Alban kings. Julius Cæsar, who was descended from them, is said to have always worn it.

The cothurnus, very like the mulleus, is distinguished by a leather strap passing between the big toe and the others. It usually appears on representations of Diana, and many examples (also of the mulleus) are to be seen on paintings discovered at Herculaneum.

The phæcasium was a boot of white leather covering the entire foot, worn by women and such characters as Petronius.

The pero, according to Virgil, was a boot of rough leather or untanned hide, said to have been originally worn by senators. However, from the time of Caius Marius, 157-86 B.C., their boot was high, black, with an ornament of silver or ivory formed like a letter "C" or a crescent moon. This gave rise to the name "calcei lunati" (crescent-shaped shoes). The descendants of the one hundred senators appointed by Romulus were permitted to wear crescents on the shoe, above the heel and behind the ankle.

The caliga was the stout, spike-soled shoe of the soldiers.

Sandals in museums reveal a great variety in style and open leather work. During the Empire the shoes of the women were elaborately ornamented with pearls, gold, silver, precious stones and embroidery.

Headgear.—The petasus or wide-brimmed Thessalonian hat (see the Greeks), was assumed by Romans of the better class when making a journey. The pileus, a cone-shaped hat tightly fitting the head, was worn by the common people, especially at the feast of the Saturnalia; this was also the head covering of freed slaves.

The Hair.—The Romans wore their hair curled and waved, though the statues give us the impression of greater rigidity and more elaborate formation than shown on those of the Greeks. It was necessary to use false hair made up in braided forms to achieve some of the effects. Horace calls one of these erections the caliendrum. The vitta, a band of ribbon bound about the heads of maidens, was affected by the more staid and respectable, according to Ovid. Priests and priestesses, also sacrificial victims, were so decorated.

During the Empire the hair was not only painted yellow with saffron but sprinkled with gold dust.

The men (according to Pliny) were bearded until 454 B.C., and most of the emperors clean shaven. At the first indication of the advent of a beard, a boy went through the ceremonial of its dedication to a god. The Romans wore uncut hair in times of mourning.

The Caul.—The caul, a fashion often resurrected

throughout the ages, is a net on the hair of gold wire, pearled and jeweled, and sometimes embroidered.

Jewels and Ornamentation.—Borders, with repeated designs over the center of the goods following the Greek fashion, were used. Jewelry was lavishly displayed; rings, made like the bracelets and armlets in many varieties of metal, were worn by men and women of low and high degree. Twisted gold wires were used both in rings and armlets. Rings with intaglios served as official seals for their owners' legal papers. Women wore necklaces and long earrings set with precious stones; armlets and bracelets often represented serpents. Pins with large ornamental heads of intricate designs were used for sticking in the coiffure.

Cicero says the "fasciola" was a purple band placed about the ankle by women.

On his return from a victorious campaign, a hero, marching from the Campus Martius to the Capitol, wore a wreath of laurel denoting the people's recognition of his services. Julius Cæsar obtained permission from the Senate to adopt the fashion for himself. On old coins we find the Cæsars wearing laurel wreaths tied about the head with loops of ribbon.

The Bulla.—A golden ball, mentioned by Juvenal and of Etruscan origin, was suspended about the neck of noble Roman boys until the age of fourteen; it was sometimes of a heart shape and contained charms to ward off evil. It was worn also by triumphant generals. In Beerbohm Tree's production of "Nero," heart-shaped bullæ decorated the necks of both Acte and Octavia, the young girls of the play.

ROMAN ARMOR AND MILITARY DRESS

The Lorica.—A cuirass, originally of leather, was made so that it followed the form of the body. The same idea was carried out later in metal of elaborate design. The statue of Augustus Cæsar in the Vatican, and the one of Trajan at Naples, show closely fitting loricas adorned with figures of gods. Underneath were double tunics with wide pleats showing at the shoulders and above the knees, the fullness of the material easing the pressure of the metal.

The Paludamentum.—A cloak, longer but corresponding to the Grecian chlamys, was draped over the shoulder, arm and chest. One is shown on the statue of Julius Cæsar in the Capitoline Museum, in Rome.

The Paragonium.—A short sword was fastened to the cinctura (belt).

Brass helmets were topped by variously colored horsehair crests.

The buskin or cothurnus was worn by generals; the caliga, by common soldiers; greaves on the legs.

One division of infantry, the Velites, wore the skins of wolves over the head; they were armed with swords, light javelins and bucklers (shields) of a circular form three feet in diameter.

The Hastiti, composed of older men, used a convex shield two by four feet, made of two planks fastened together and covered with linen and calfskin, with a boss (knob) of iron on its center; brass helmets with three feathers either black or red; a brass pectoral or a ringed lorica. (This resembled the one worn by Normans.)

The Principes and the Triarii carried pikes instead of javelins.

The Standard Bearers draped the head and skin of a lion over their head and shoulders. The image of an eagle appeared on the standards; those of Brutus and Caius were of silver.

THE THEATRE

The Romans, like the Greeks, used masks in theatrical productions. Actors wearing them entertained the public at festivals and impersonated the dead at funerals. During the reign of Tiberius all players were banished from Rome.

The Gladiators.—All those who fought in the arena of an amphitheatre were called gladiators. First known in Rome, 264 B.C., this class represented condemned criminals, slaves and desperate characters who gained a precarious prolongation of existence by fighting wild beasts. Before the fall of the Empire these combats had become such a fad that even senators and emperors entered the arena.

The gladiatorial costumes are depicted on the wall paintings found at Pompeii. Every form of known weapon was used. The retiarii carried nets and tridents, fillets bound the hair, the entire left side including the shoulder and arm was protected by armor, the caliga covering the foot. The secutores, whose business necessitated their being as light as possible on the feet in order to avoid being ensnared in the net, used no body armor save on the right arm; the subligaculum (an apron), sandals, a tight-fitting helmet and a large round shield completed the costume. The two classes known as velis and

samnis wore a red or white subligaculum held by a girdle
of bronze or embroidered leather; the rest of their equip-
ment was made up of a buskin of colored leather worn on
the right leg with a greave on the left, a helmet with ornamental visor, a long buckler and thigh armor of iron
plates. Gladiators who hailed from Thrace were clad in
their native armor.

Edwin Forrest as Spartacus, in Robert Montgomery
Bird's tragedy, "The Gladiator," is represented on an old
engraving in a leather lorica, a gold-fringed tunic and
buskins. His face is decorated with side whiskers, mustache and a lip beard. No matter what the part, Hamlet,
Othello, Macbeth, Coriolanus and even Metamora, the Indian chief, Forrest never sacrificed these facial trimmings
so fashionable in the nineteenth century.

The Charioteers.—There were four sections distin-
guishable by the color of the costumes, *viz.,* blue, green,
red or white. Thongs clasped about a short tunic gave
extra support to the body; the long reins were wound
about the waist and hips with a short knife, its blade
shaped somewhat like a question mark, thrust through
them to use for cutting loose in case of accident. In the
photoplay "Ben Hur," this detail is omitted; both Navarro
and Bushman wear knives in their corselets of leather
strappings, but the reins, beyond the loop through which
they are held by the drivers, are allowed to dangle loosely
to the floor of the chariot. The *raison d'être* for the knife
was, apparently, overlooked.

Augustus Cæsar became the first Emperor of Rome in
27 B.C. At this date Virgil, Horace, Livy and Ovid were
living.

Rome fell in the fifth century, A.D.

CHAPTER XI

THE FRANKS, GOTHS, GAULS, CELTS, TEUTONS, LOMBARDS AND ANCIENT BRITONS

FTER the fall of Rome the costumes worn in Italy, Spain and France underwent a change. From having been pure Roman they became, like their wearers, Italian, Spanish and French. By the ninth century, Latin had become a dead language among these people commonly called the Romance nations.

Of the wild men responsible, the Ostrogoths, who defeated the Emperor of Western Rome, were overthrown by Justinian, Emperor of the East in 544; the Visigoths (West Goths), who possessed Southern Gaul and the greater part of Spain, were driven south of the Pyrenees by the Franks, who in turn were conquered by the Moors. The Arabs held most of Spain from 711 to 1492 when they were driven from Granada by Ferdinand and Isabella.

The Franks laid the foundation of the French nation; Clovis, their leader, was victorious at Soissons in 486, forever destroying in Gaul the Roman authority which had existed since Julius Cæsar enforced it on the natives five centuries before. The Franks were known as Merovingians from 486 to 752, when a new royal line, the Carolingian, was established.

THE FRANKS

Leg Gartering.—Strips of leather crisscrossed about the leg, usually to the knee but occasionally to the thigh, held cloth or crudely made trousers to the leg. The early costume of the Franks consisted of long trousers either gathered about the ankles or strapped with leg gartering, sandals or bare feet, tunics and hooded cloaks. Later, during the reign of the Carolingians, long, full tunics were draped with voluminous mantles, both displaying wide borders.

THE GOTHS

Men.—Knee-length tunics were placed over trousers. These garments, together with a cloak worn knotted in front, were cut about the edges in long points, a style distinctly Gothic. Long hair and beards were the rule.

Women.—A double tunic was arranged with the right shoulder and breast uncovered; bare feet and long flying hair accompanied it.

THE GAULS

The Gauls are described as follows by Diodorus Siculus, a companion of Cæsar: "The Gauls wear bracelets about their wrists and arms, and massy chains of pure and beaten gold about their necks and weighty rings upon their fingers, and corselets of gold upon their breasts. For stature they are tall, of a pale complexion, and red haired, not only naturally, but they endeavor all they can to make it redder by art. They often wash their hair in water boiled with lime, and turn it backwards from the forehead to the crown of the head, and thence to their very necks, that their faces may be fully seen. . . . Some of them shave their beards, others let them grow a little. Persons of quality shave their chins close, but their mustaches they let fall so low that they even cover their mouths. . . . Their garments are very strange, for they wear parti-colored tunics, flowered with various colors in divisions and hose which they call bracæ. They likewise wear checkered sagas [cloaks]. Those they wear in winter are thick, those in summer more slender. Upon their heads they wear helmets of brass with large appendages made for ostentation's sake to be admired by the beholders. . . . They have trumpets after the barbarian manner, which in sounding make a horrid noise . . . for swords they use a broad weapon called Spatha, which they hang across their right thigh by iron or brazen chains. Some gird themselves with belts of gold and silver." (From a translation used by Charles Knight.)

That the Gauls made striped and checkered materials and were expert dyers is vouched for by Pliny. When stripes were used they ran diagonally across the garments. Roman sculptures show long trousers, the bracæ, gathered about the ankle, and high shoes.

The costuming of the Gauls should always be colorful.

Men.—The men wore a checked or striped tunic; trousers, the saga, either fastened with a clasp on the right shoulder or cut with a round hole in the middle through which the head was passed; a broad heavy sword hanging over the right hip; gold corselets, helmets and belts with the usual barbaric array of jewelry in the form of neckbands, armlets, rings and bracelets of twisted wire called torques.

Women.—The women wore two tunics, one long to the

feet, the other reaching to the hips and confined under the bust by a girdle. The hair hung in long braids over each shoulder.

THE CELTS

Men.—Long and short tunics, cloaks made with a hole to pass the head through, and buskins to the knee were worn by the men. The mantles and edges of skirts were cut in points, much smaller, however, than those decorating the garments of the Goths. Saffron was a popular color. It was a Celtic fashion to rush naked into battle.

Women.—Fitted bodices, full skirts, bare feet, and hair parted in the middle characterized the women's costume.

THE TEUTONS OR GERMANS

They roamed the section between the Rhine and the Danube.

Men.—The hair of the primitive type was tied up on top of the head, thence falling loose; they were mostly naked, the costume being merely a garment resembling trunks. Later (the Germans were barbaric until the sixth century) long trousers were worn under a sleeved tunic reaching to the knee, a draped cloak on one shoulder. Stripes appeared as border decoration; there was also a fashion of running two across the chest. Tunics were slit up the sides and girdled with ropes or leather. Armlets, anklets, caps and sandals were all of leather. The armor consisted of a cuirass worn over the tunic, a large circular shield, arrows in a quiver, a sword and a helmet of metal over a leather cap. The cloak was fastened to the right shoulder.

PLATE VII. EARLY CHRISTIANS, ARABS AND NORSEMEN

A and B. Byzantine emperor and a lady.
C and D. A Roman Christian, 600 A.D., and a Christian martyr.
E and F. An Arab girl and a sheik in haik and burnous.
G. and H. A Gaul and a Viking.

Women.—Garments were fastened over one shoulder, the other being left bare like those of the Goths. . Sandals were of openwork leather.

THE LOMBARDS

A barbarian tribe from Germany which conquered a large part of Italy, 568-774. At the latter date Charlemagne, the most noted Carolingian ruler, was victorious over them. Their blood still exists in Lombardy, fair hair and light complexions revealing a German strain. Their clothes were barbarically splendid.

Men.—The men wore tunics, large mantles, leg gartering over cloth and pointed shoes.

Women.—A long, full tunic with wide sleeves ended in embroidered and jeweled borders; an inner gown showed a sleeve tight to the wrist, and over all was worn a large mantle. The hair, parted in the middle, was adorned with crowns and diadems from which veils floated.

THE ANCIENT BRITONS

To the writings and letters of Cæsar and his companions during the conquest of Britain we are indebted for much light on the costuming of its inhabitants. We must believe that in battle they appeared almost naked, their bodies colored blue by the application of woad, a plant of the mustard family whose leaves when ground supplied this stain. All these authorities unite in finding a great similarity in manners and costume between the Britons and the Gauls. Pliny says they excelled in both weaving and dyeing. Fine wool dyed purple, scarlet and other colors was spun into yarn which was woven to produce checks or stripes. It is believed these secrets were discovered by the Gauls, who imparted them to the Britons. The tartan of the Highlanders is called the "garb of old Gaul."

The costume consisted of the usual cloak of fur or cloth, a tunic (Dion Cassius states that the one worn by Boadicea, Queen of Ancient Britain, was "in several colors all in folds") and the leather leg strappings over skins or cloth. The primitive shoe was of skin gathered about the ankles. The men were bearded, the hair of both sexes falling on the shoulders. They wore barbaric jewelry in the form of necklaces, armlets and bracelets of twisted wire called torques, and rings of gold, silver, brass and bronze. Pliny says a ring was worn on the middle finger. A king had golden bands about the neck, arms and knees as emblems of supreme authority. Old armor in the form of battle-axes, bronze swords and round bronze shields is found in collections. After the Roman Conquest the last named were oblong in form.

King Arthur and his Knights of the Round Table (*viz.*, Lancelot, Tristram, Gawaine and Galahad) were semi-legendary heroes.

Of the three divisions of Druids, the ovates or sacred musicians and religious poets wore green; the bards or historians and genealogical poets, blue; and those who performed the duties of priests, white.

CHAPTER XII

THE CHRISTIANS: ROMANS, BYZANTINES AND THE MONKS

THE ROMAN CHRISTIANS

URING the early period the Christians known as Nazarenes wore Grecian tunics and the pallium. The marble Saint Cecelia, lying on her side as though sleeping in the Catacombs of Saint Calixtus at Rome, wears a long-sleeved tunic, a girdle and a veil which completely covers her head.

The long tunics and mantles were superseded in the fifth century as follows:

Men.—The men wore cloaks fastened to the right shoulder; a knee-length tunic; trousers with a broad stripe down the front tucked into laced buskins.

Women.—The women used tunics, fringed and bordered; wide sleeves; a white girdle, very long with the ends brought up in folds over the left shoulder. The rich indulged in jewels and clothes of fine material.

THE BYZANTINES

The Empire of the East with its capitol at Constantinople, after 328, ceased to be Roman and was called Greek or Byzantine. The influence of the East began immediately to show itself upon the civilization and the costumes.

400-700

Men.—Knee-length tunics with checked girdles were fastened high under the armpits; trousers extended either to below the knees where they were met by buskins, or were cut short, allowing the knee and several inches above to show. Knots and drapes of material were placed as decoration on the trouser ends and at the top of the buskin. For soldiers, a cuirass with knee pants showing beneath it, and greaves on the bare legs sufficed.

Women.—The hair was confined in a most distinctive mode, a rolled pompadour being wound with ribbons, also ornamented with pearls and jewels. Long strings of pearls, each terminating with a large one of a pear shape, fell from the hair over the shoulders, and long earrings of pear-shaped pearls were worn. This was a fashion of Byzantine origin.

A large square cloak having a hole through which the head was passed fell in four points, each weighted with tassels. Checked borders were much used.

A long-sleeved tunic was finished by a wide border in varied colors, and reached to the floor. Flowered effects, also leaves, appeared in all-over designs on silk (a material more favored than wool by the Byzantines). The girdle, a band of white about three inches wide with one long fringed end, hung to the bottom of the gown in front.

Theodora, wife of Justinian, Emperor of the East, 483-565, belongs to the period just described. She should be costumed in voluminous and rich clothes, and not appear half naked as in the movies.

By 700 ornamentation greatly increased. Tunics developed a loose, wide sleeve allowing the tight one of an

inner gown of contrasting color to show at the wrist.
Women wore large jeweled ornaments behind each ear,
and parted the hair in the middle.

A curious decoration in the form of rectangular plaques
embroidered, jeweled and of diversified color, was applied to the borders of enormous cloaks.

There was much color in the costume; knee-length
tunics covered with embroidery in brilliant hues were
worn over long white ones.

All shields and spears were marked with the monogram
of Christ; the vestments were very elaborate.

1000-1200

A wide panel of material heavily jeweled, encircling the
shoulders and descending in front nearly to the edges of
the robe, was worn by the emperor, empress and nobles.
Pearls were suspended from the hair of women and sewn
to the edges of their garments. Crosses depending from
ropes of pearl were fastened in the hair, which once more
offered a distinctive style. A braid was made close behind each ear, a tight-fitting caul of gold and pearls placed
on the head, and the two braids then carried up from the
back of the neck over the crown to the forehead, where
they disappeared beneath a jeweled band. Another headdress differed only in that the hair was rolled with ribbons instead of braided. These styles were used subsequently in Germany.

The Asiatic influence showed largely in the men's
clothes. Phrygian caps were in evidence, also trousers
with stripes and patterns running spirally up the leg.

Byzantine costumes of the fourth century are correct
for the "Comedy of Errors."

PLATE VIII. BYZANTINE AND GERMAN HEADDRESSES

A, B and C. Headdresses of Byzantine women (after Hottenroth).
D, E and F. Headdresses of German women during the fourteenth
century, showing an oriental tendency (after Hottenroth).

The Monks.—An Egyptian ascetic, born 251 and later known as Saint Anthony, was copied by thousands of religious enthusiasts; men who consecrated their lives to the service of Christ as missionaries and teachers were known as monks and from the third to the sixth century founded many monasteries in Europe, thus spreading Christianity and civilization, and having a tremendous influence on costume. Their own has always been a wide-sleeved and cowled tunic of coarse cloth held by a rope girdle. Some orders wore over it a scapulary, *i.e.,* a garment cut like a surcoat which reached to the hem of the undergarment. The foot was either bare or shod with a simple leather sandal.

The best known followers of Saint Anthony were:

Saint Benedict, 480-543, who founded the famous Benedictine monastery known as Monte Cassino, between Rome and Naples;

A priest called Patricius, who converted Ireland before his death in 469 and became known as Saint Patrick, beloved of the Irish;

Saint Augustine, who in 496 was sent by the Pope to England with forty other monks as companions and was successful in converting the Britons from the worship of Woden and Thor;

Saint Boniface, 688-753, who converted Germany.

All of these monks directly influenced dress by subduing the barbaric and introducing the civilized. Indeed, to two missionary monks returning from a pilgrimage to China, Europe was indebted for its first silk in 533 A.D.

Mongol-Chinese numbering 700,000, led by Attila the Hun, were driven back into Asia after their defeat at the battle of Chalons, 442 A.D., thus saving Europeans from pigtails and oriental dress.

In 711 the Saracens conquered Spain, which they held for eight hundred years. They attempted to follow up this victory by subduing France, but were overwhelmingly defeated at the battle of Tours, 732, by the Franks under the leadership of Charles Martel. France was saved not only from the Turks but from their trousers.

Charlemagne reigned 768-814. He was victorious over the greater part of western Europe and the Pope rewarded him with the Imperial crown of the Cæsars. To him is accredited the founding of modern civilization. The French people immediately started on their long career as dictators of the mode.

CHAPTER XIII

THE ANGLO-SAXONS AND THE VIKINGS

THE ANGLO-SAXONS

HE Saxons were in England after 450 and established a monarchy which lasted six hundred years.

MEN

The Trousers.—These were long, loose, and strapped to the leg by a cross-gartering of cloth, linen or leather which sometimes extended to the thigh. They gradually assumed a closer form until tights were evolved in the tenth century. Cross-gartering, however, was retained until the thirteenth.

The Tunic.—This was usually knee length and opened downward from each hip for freer movement. The edges were embroidered or woven in colored thread to form a border. Very long sleeves formed a series of rolls above the wrist, where a bracelet kept them from slipping over the hand. Girdles were worn with both long and short tunics. The former were for men of dignity, all edges being decorated with embroidery or fur.

The word "gunna" (called Saxon by some, but probably Norman, as "gune" is old French for gown) is supposed to apply to the long full tunic of both sexes. The "cyrtle" or kirtle is generally understood to mean the inner gown or tunic.

The Mantle.—One variety had an opening for the head

PLATE IX. DETAILS OF COSTUMES FOR HAMLET

A. Costume worn by Edwin Forrest as Hamlet (from an old photograph).

B. Black tunic edged with white about the neck worn by Walter Hampden and resembling that of Edwin Booth (detail after a *Times World Wide* photograph).

C. Correct sleeves on the tunic of John Barrymore (detail after a photograph by Bruguière).

D. Leg-strapping as worn by Edwin Booth (detail from a photograph by Gurney and Co.).

E and F. Border design and shoe used by Charles Fechter (from a gravure by Gebbie and Co.).

and was looped up over the arms with a section falling in folds somewhat like a chasuble. Others clasped in front or on the shoulder.

Footgear.—Low leather shoes were slashed over the instep like sandals and sometimes attached to the cross-gartering. Socks were worn inside the shoes over stockings with ornamental bands about the tops.

Hair.—The Anglo-Saxon beard was full and cut in two points, the hair hanging to the collar line. Specimens of very large double combs have been found.

Armor of chains, rings or scales formed a garment called a coat of mail; the Saxon boss on the shield rose six or seven inches in height.

WOMEN

The girdle was placed rather high under the bust with the gown pulled up through it in front, allowing the kirtle to show. This gave a thick, bunchy appearance not so noticeable several centuries later when the same trick was used with a girdle placed low about the hips.

The Wimple.—The hair was worn loose, or in braids, bound by a fillet about the brow, that for an unmarried girl being known as a snood. The wimple, which became an established mode in the ninth century, was a large square of white linen or colored cloth laid over the head with one end thrown around the neck in such a manner as to completely hide all hair from view. It was sometimes broad enough to drape the shoulders like a wrap, or to hang as a veil with a gold or jeweled band holding it about the brow.

Large, circular earrings were worn. Women's shoes were tied or buckled about the ankles.

The Anglo-Saxons were skillful in the spinning of flax; they also understood the art of dyeing. A strong cloth of superior quality was called "stamfortis." The furs in use were sable, beaver, fox, cat and lamb.

THE VIKINGS

In the times of Sweyn, King of Denmark, 981, and of Canute, 1027, also of the Norsemen, the costume for the men was at once picturesque and barbaric. Buskins of leather were strapped on bare legs or over gray woolen stockings. The knees were always bare. Coats of mail were worn over short-sleeved, knee-length tunics of dull color. The skins of wild animals draped the whole: a leopard skin over one shoulder with the head close to the ear, or a gray wolfskin with its head hanging down the back. Armlets of copper or brass on bare arms, and helmets of shining metal in striking designs decorated with bull's horns or surmounted by towering eagle wings completed the costume.

For Canute, a helmet of silver bound round by a golden band and crested by a golden dragon is correct. A gold-bordered red mantle should be suspended from the shoulders and cut to sweep the ground. A corselet of leather, completely studded with gold plates, is worn over a short tunic. According to the sagas, also old MSS., Canute wore over his tunic a long mantle fastened with cords and tassels. His shoes are described as being high with embroidered bands about the top, a form of buskin. His body when exhumed in 1766 was found decorated with gold and silver bands, one encircling his head, a jeweled ring on one finger. In the *Knyghtlinga Saga,* his hair is described as luxuriant.

The mustaches worn by the Norsemen should hang to the chest. Saxon beards were very common.

Women.—The women wore the wimple and a gown like the Saxon.

Hamlet.—The dress of the Dane in the tenth and eleventh centuries, according to Strutt, resembled the Anglo-Saxon's. Black was a favorite color, although one writer in 1127 states that they had become wearers of "scarlet, purple and fine linen." Another speaks of them as "effeminately gay in their dress," spending much time caring for their hair, which hung in flowing ringlets. Scarlet was the color originally worn by royalty. Hamlet as prince of the blood should have been robed in it, which, according to Charles Knight, accounts for the objections of the Queen and Claudius to his dressing in black. This, although a popular color, did not represent mourning, as the Danes wore none. Blanche Yurka, playing the Queen to John Barrymore's Hamlet, was a stunning figure garbed in royal scarlet.

Besides the coat of mail, the Danes used a tunic of quilted cloth called a panzar (this was later of metal), made to protect the lower part of the body and especially the abdomen. The national weapon was the bipennis, or double-headed axe. The helmet had a nose guard to which the collar of the mail hood could be hooked; only the eyes were left unguarded.

CHAPTER XIV

THE NORMAN PERIOD AND SCOTTISH DRESS

WILLIAM THE CONQUEROR, 1066-1087

MEN

HE Tunic.—The costume closely resembles the Anglo-Saxon: a loose tunic either gathered to the waist by a band or fitting closely to the knees with an opening up each side to the hip to allow of free movement; the neck slit open in a V called the vente to a depth of five inches, its edges embroidered in bright colors as were those of the wide elbow-length sleeves.

The Shirt.—This garment was white and worn under the tunic, with very long sleeves pushed up as on the Saxon dress, forming a series of folds above the wrist. The vente was filled under by the shirt.

Chausses.—Roughly fashioned tights of wool were bound to the leg by cross-garterings of leather or cord; some were held in at the ankle and knee by bands. Girdles of leather encircled the waist to support the sword.

The Mantle.—The mantle was semicircular and fastened to the right shoulder or at the front by a large brooch. Some were held together by drawing a fold of material through a ring attached to the shoulder.

After the Conquest, ermine, squirrel, marten, rabbit and goat augmented the list of furs in use in England.

Footgear.—Yellow, blue, green and red shoes, with rolled over tops faced with colored bands, fitted the foot to above the ankle; the toes were slightly twisted.

Hats.—Of the cap variety, some hats were round and brimless, others rose to a peak in the center of the crown; one shape duplicated the Phrygian with its forward turned peak. Hoods were often worn under the helmet.

The Hair.—Faces were clean shaven and hair cropped close; that of the king shaved at the back of his neck.

WOMEN

The costume in general was like that of the men. The tunic with wide elbow-length sleeves was very long and held in place by an often richly ornamented girdle through which it was sometimes pulled up to the knee, allowing a long white undergown to show; this latter garment was finished with wrinkled sleeve ends and supplied a filling like a vestee for the neck opening.

A wimple or "couvre-chef," completely covering the hair, was wound about the throat and shoulders and held to the brow by a fillet.

Mittens were in use.

Peasants wore canvas and coarse fustian, a cloth very popular among the Normans. The bliaut or bliausis mentioned in old romances is supposed to have been a long garment resembling a smock, bliaut and the modern French word blouse probably having some connection, according to Planché; in the Middle Ages it took the form of the surcoat.

Say was a worsted cloth used for stockings (from the Dutch "sasijet," worsted).

PLATE X. NORMANS, SAXONS AND FRANKS

A, B and C. Normans.
D and E. Saxons.
F and I. Franks of the peasant and middle class.
G and H. Eleventh century. A Carolingian king and lady.

The favored colors seem to have been red, blue and green.

WILLIAM II, 1087-1100

Sleeves became so long it was necessary to turn them back over the wrists; shoes developed long pointed toes which were stuffed with wool; a general tendency to lengthen all parts of the dress was noticeable. Loose tights were left unbound except at the ankle. Beards and mustaches were worn.

WOMEN

The tunic was laced up the back, the idea of making the dress fit the figure snugly having spread from the women of the Continent.

Cloaks were amply cut, lined with fur and hung from the shoulders by straps across the bosom.

HENRY I, 1100-1135

MEN

Long tunics reaching to the feet were beginning to make their appearance. Sleeves touched the ground; it was necessary to knot them up to prevent treading on them. Long slits were cut at the elbow through which the arm emerged, the rest of the sleeve hanging down.

Tights began to shape more to the leg, but were still confined by cross-gartering and covered to the knees by the tunic.

Stockings were worn under the long tunics by both men and women. The crooked point on the shoe grew longer. Beards were long, the hair hanging in curls.

Round crowned hats had fairly wide brims and a knob on top.

Armor of chain, rings or scales, known as mail, was worn until superseded by full plate in 1300.

The manufacture of woolens is first mentioned in 1111 after some Flemish refugees sought shelter in England.

WOMEN

Cases.—The wimple went out of style and two apparently long and thick braids appeared reaching to the knee, or the gown's hem. This wealth of hair was achieved by braiding in ribbons and false hair (as in a Chinese queue), or by the use of "cases," devices of metal or gaily colored silks fastened to the end of the natural hair. They were of various length and finished off either with long tassels or a braid of false hair.

Note that exaggerations in fashion, such as the very long sleeves, hair, etc., were not followed by the poorer classes. Linen wimples were used by peasant women for several hundred years.

STEPHEN, 1135-1154

The costume was practically the same as for preceding reign. Pointed shoes took on eccentric shapes, resembling ram's horns, scorpion tails, and the like.

THE SCOTCH

Macbeth.—King Duncan was killed in 1039 and Dunsinane taken in 1054. The famous portrait by Sargent of Ellen Terry as Lady Macbeth shows her with two long braids bound with ribbons. As this fashion was not followed in England until the twelfth century, the Scottish

lady must have copied her style from the women of the
Continent who used it in the eleventh century. In knowl-
edge of the mode she would have been considerably in
advance of her English neighbors. Clare Eames, when
playing the part in support of Hackett, wore her hair
parted in the middle from forehead to nape of neck,
braided in two and wound about each ear as was the fashion for young girls several years ago before they went
mad over the bob. In the banquet scene, Miss Eames
wore a wimple of thin white gauze about her cheeks, chin
and throat; a red chiffon veil tied over her head concealed
all hair and hung to the floor. On top of all was placed a
crown. This was correct according to the Anglo-Saxon
and Norman fashion prevalent in England at the time.
In her train, one lady in waiting was allowed to appear
with her hair in two long braids.

James K. Hackett as Macbeth wore very long mustaches, a Saxon beard cut in two points and long red hair
falling on his shoulders. He used two tunics, one long
and the other short; the former was worn sometimes underneath, when of a dark color; sometimes outside and
slit open to the hips, revealing the inner tunic. Leg-
strappings reached to the knee with the upper part of leg
bare, until the last act when dark green woolen tights
were bound at the knee. With this last costume he wore
the Saxon shirt of ring mail and a brass helmet like that
of the Gaul and Dane. A single broad eagle's feather is
worn in the bonnet of a Highland chieftain and Hackett
like most of his predecessors in the part since any attention at all has been paid to correct theatrical costuming, so
decorated his.

All cloaks were fastened to the shoulders with large

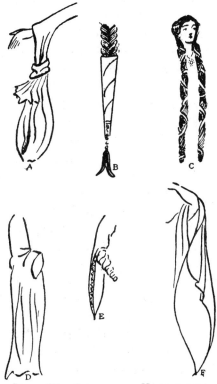

PLATE XI.   SLEEVES AND HAIRDRESSING

A. Long sleeve knotted up, England, Henry I.

B. A case for lengthening the hair.

C. Ribbon bound hair in Sargent's portrait of Ellen Terry as Lady Macbeth.

D. Long hanging sleeves, England, Henry I.

E. Sleeve of a Norman tunic, showing wrinkled shirt sleeve on the forearm.

F. Sleeve worn by Ellen Terry as Lady Macbeth in the Sargent portrait.

circular ornaments; this permitted of much graceful draping of the folds over the left arm, also the ever stunning
effect created by drawing one end from the right side (as
with the toga) and throwing it over the left shoulder.

The shield was round and covered with bull's hide, the
fur being white and light tan. In the center was a knob
of brass. It was held by thrusting the arm through straps
placed on its inner side. (Most shields are so constructed.)

The Scottish weapons of the eleventh century, besides
the round shield which was studded with nails and bosses
of brass and iron, included the claymore (a two-handled
and double-edged broadsword) and the dirk or "bidag."
The king and his chieftains wore the shirt of ring mail or
copied the quilted panzar of the Norwegians and Danes.
It is said that most of the Highlanders followed the old
Celtic fashion of rushing into battle nearly naked.

The costume of the women followed lines prevalent
among the Anglo-Saxons and Normans of the day: a
long tunic confined by a girdle at the waist, a mantle fastened in front by a large brooch of gold, silver or brass set
with precious stones or the pebbles of the country, which
when highly polished are very ornamental, owing to their
varied colorings and crystal clearness. A stone known as
the "cairngorm" has always been popular in Scotland.

A very ancient garment for women was known as the
"arisaid." It has been described as checked, also as
striped—white with yellow. The women of the Hebrides,
according to Strutt, always wore this capacious mantle
which trailed on the floor unless its superfluous length
was caught up about the waist by a belt of leather trimmed
with silver to resemble a chain; a plate about eight inches
long by three wide, engraved or set with crystals or coral,

was attached to the long ends of the tongue. It was still used in 1740.

Several other articles of Scottish clothing date back to very remote days. The long-sleeved, saffron-stained shirt of Irish origin—the sleeves also enormously wide—was worn under a short woolen jacket with open sleeves. The "truis" or "trowse," a long wide pantaloon corded about the waist in use among the ancient Irish and corresponding to the trousers of the Gauls, has been traced in Scotland as far back as 1538. Authorities, including Charles Knight, hold, however, that as all chiefs of great Celtic and Gaelic families wore this leg covering it is quite probable that the ancient Scottish chieftains did likewise. Nevertheless, we always conjure up a mental picture of a hardy Scot whose bare legs are covered only by the kilt and sporran augmented sometimes by stockings and buskins. Why try to make the men "wha hae wi' Wallace bled" more delicate than their descendants?

Perhaps the most famous part of the Scottish costume was the plaid, a shaggy woolen rug thrown over the body and belted about the waist. That combination known as "Shepherd's Plaid" is supposed to be the oldest, possibly antedating the process of dyeing, the natural black and white wool of the sheep being utilized. The distinguishing plaids of various clans are said to be of later date, only those of the higher classes being in colors. "Plaid" originally meant the garment itself while the woolen stuff of which it was made was called "tartan."

CHAPTER XV

FROM CHARLEMAGNE TO THE THIRTEENTH CENTURY

THE CAROLINGIANS: CHARLEMAGNE, 768-814

HE King is represented in a long tunic, a voluminous mantle fastened to his right shoulder, a crown set on long hair, bushy mustaches and a long beard divided in two sections. Borders appeared on all garments.

Short bordered tunics, cloth-wrappings fastened to the leg by leather cross-gartering with sandals attached, mantles of cloth or skins hanging from the shoulders, Phrygian caps, long hair reaching to the shoulders and mustaches that swept the chest were worn.

Women had long gowns held to the figure by rope girdles with tasseled ends, and long wimples confined about the brow by circlets of gold over flowing hair.

THE NINTH AND TENTH CENTURIES
Men

The dress lost its barbaric look: full length tights with a V-shaped kilt, much decorated and hanging over them to the knees in front were added. A three-quarter length cloak fastened on the breast by a clasp and elaborately bordered; a Phrygian cap and low shoes of leather completed the costume.

THE ELEVENTH CENTURY

The Tunic.—The men wore two; one reaching to the calf allowed a full one of another color to show below. Sandals had leg-strappings attached. The tunic of the Italian women was fastened to fit the figure closely. The women of France and Germany wore a corselet over the tunic; this was laced up the back and resembled an early twentieth-century corset. In England the gown itself was laced. An embroidered girdle was wound twice around the hips and fastened low in front with long hanging ends. All dresses trailed on the floor, long sleeves were knotted up, veils or wimples were suspended from the head. Braids bound with ribbon appeared nearly a century sooner than in England. A woman with any pretension to rank wore a crown; this had a wimple or veil (volet) draped over it.

The Knight Templars.—They carried triangular shields with rounded tops almost as long as the body of the bearer, and decorated with a cross.

Long coats of mail (hauberks) slashed about the skirts for freedom, were worn over full-length tunics of cloth. On the breast was a large cross. Helmets were shaped like the Phrygian cap. A scabbard containing a mighty sword was suspended from a broad belt.

In this century Peter the Hermit, a famous monk, lived in France. It was the time of the Cid in Spain.

THE TWELFTH CENTURY

Silk was manufactured at Palermo, 1130.

Abelard and Héloïse lived in France early in the century.

The Surcot, Old French (in English, Surcoat).—This was a piece of goods twice the length of the body from neck to ankle and sufficiently wide to reach well over the shoulders. In its center a round hole was cut through which the head passed; the sides were left open, the front sometimes slashed from ankle to knee. A leather belt with a long tongue descended to the edge of the garment confining its fullness about the waist. The surcoat was worn over the tunic, now ankle length; it was quickly adopted in Italy, France, Germany and England. Fur lined it in winter; it was also worn over armor.

Large mantles were decorated with rectangular plaques about the edges after the Byzantine fashion.

The *aumônière* was a pouch or handbag suspended from a woman's girdle.

Spanish women, ever under the influence of the Arabs, wore a turbaned headdress.

THE ENGLISH: HENRY II, 1154-1189

The Plantagenet period, commonly spoken of as the Middle Ages, commenced.

MEN

Clothes retained the same general cut as in the two preceding reigns. Richer material was used, and the tights became well shaped to the leg, with cross-garterings ending in tassels below the knee. Shoes were of colored leather, not black, with gold stripes as decoration.

WOMEN

The Chin Band.—An extremely flattering fashion for a lady who was "getting on," introduced when face lifting was unknown. The hair again went into concealment and the headdress, by passing a band of linen under the chin, securing it to another bound about the brow, the whole covered with a linen wimple, bore a strong resemblance to that of the modern nun.

Shoes had a blunt toe bent back over the foot, the fastening consisting of one button above the ankle. Both these and the high boots reaching to the calf were rolled over at the top, displaying a colored lining.

Gloves with jeweled backs were worn by the wealthy and woolen mittens by the poor.

Fair Rosamund, the favorite of the king and the most romantic figure of the time, should appear in the costume of this reign.

RICHARD I (CŒUR DE LION), 1189-1199

MEN

Two tunics were worn, the under one reaching the ground; these were belted with a broad girdle. The crusades were on, however, and most men, including the king, spent the greater part of that reign in the Holy Land.

WOMEN

The same dress as that for the reign of Henry II was favored. Young girls showed their hair; ribbon fillets confined it about the brow.

CHAPTER XVI

THE THIRTEENTH CENTURY

THE ITALIANS

HE most sumptuous materials were being man-ufactured: silks, velvets, gold and silver tissue. Their use quickly spread among the wealthy on the Continent.

The gowns of the women were elaborate, with long trains and sleeves that swept the ground. Wide-spreading, silk-lined mantles of velvet or brocade were covered with gold embroidery. Diaphanous veils floated over the hair, or cauls (small caps of gold and pearls) fitted on the crown of the head.

THE FRENCH

Silk and damask were being manufactured.

Dresses were as rich as those worn by the Italians and cut on flowing lines. The chin band was used in conjunction with silken veils or wimples laid over the head.

The Gorget.—A new fashion was universally adopted by women. The hair, parted in the middle and allowed to show on top, was wound over each ear into a knob. By means of fancy pins a piece of broad linen was attached to one of these, then laid around the neck and pinned to the other, enswathing the throat as with a bandage. Over one ear a rose was coyly cocked.

PLATE XII. PLANTAGENET PERIOD

A. The surcoat, England, Richard II.

B. Gorget and wimple, England, Henry III.

C. Gorget and wire cases, England, Edward II.

D. Spanish turban and chin band, with a caul on the hair, England, Henry III.

E. Cases and forehead band, England, Edward II.

F. A surcoat with train, England, Richard II.

By the end of the century, the Frenchwoman wore her gown over a snugly laced, long-sleeved inner one, the neck of which was cut very high in choker effect.

Frenchmen wore double tunics, the under one trailing on the ground; capacious mantles; and, if the rank permitted, crowns placed on bobbed hair.

The Knight Templars.—The crusaders now carried much shorter shields though still triangular in form; the coat of mail, shortened to knee length, was worn under a surcoat; the helmet took on an entire new change in shape, becoming cylindrical with a round flat top and a perforated plate, screwed on or hinged, covering the face. This last section was called the avant taille. Most of the surcoats were closed from the armpits to the hips, the rest of their length hanging open to insure freedom to the legs. The cross was emblazoned on the chest and back.

Silk was manufactured at Bruges.

THE GERMANS

MEN

Tunics reached to the knee. A surcoat had large armholes, cut in a long V-point front and back on the neck line. All edges were finished with fur. Leather belts had long tongues. The hair was worn in a full bob.

WOMEN

The wimple and forehead band were superseded by loose hair on which was placed the Spanish turban, the chin band passing over the top.

Long cloaks were secured by a cord with knotted ends running through an ornament placed each side of the front. The very full dress was made with long, wrinkled sleeves. The kirtle gown appeared at the end of the century.

THE ENGLISH: JOHN, 1199-1216

MEN

A helmet like the cylindrical one of the French was adopted. Leather armor was covered with iron rings fastened on in overlapping rows like the Roman lorica. Surcoats were placed over armor but with as yet no coats of arms emblazoned on them. Shields were triangular. The glaive, a scythelike weapon, was carried by common soldiers. The acketon, a quilted jacket of Asiatic origin, was worn under armor, buckram, a cloth stiffened with gum, being used to strengthen it.

The fashionable surcoat was placed over the extremely long tunic with the tongue of the belt hanging to below the knees in front.

The capa was a large hooded mantle of wool; its capuchon (hood) drawn over the hatted head when traveling. A wide cloak called the balandrana served as an outer wrap.

Rather tall crowned hats had brims turned up at the back and running forward to a point, a long quilled feather standing at the side. We are familiar with them in plays dealing with Robin Hood, who, with Little John, was a celebrated outlaw of the time. Felt, made from fibers of fur mixed with wool, was used for hats during the Middle Ages. Peasants always had hats and caps of felt.

The men were clean shaven, their hair curled and sometimes bound by a fillet on the brow.

Materials.—Fur was used as trimming by all classes;

ermine, vair (minniver) and gris (marten) for the wealthy, sheep and lambskin for the poor. Lettice, a fur resembling ermine, appeared in this century.

Embroidered clothes were in fashion, a design consisting of overlapping circles being prime favorite; this also appeared in gold on shoes.

Of the new materials, burnet was a brown cloth; bysine, a fine material used in mantles (disputed whether of cotton or flax); ray, a striped cloth from Flanders; damask, a rich stuff originally from Damascus, manufactured in Sicily in the twelfth century and shortly afterward imported by England (a coarse variety called "dornix" was used for table linen).

The poorer classes had burel, a coarse brown cloth; birrhus, a coarse thick woolen cloth (an ancient hooded garment made of red wool was called a "birrhus"); bassell, sheepskin tanned.and prepared as leather, and brocella, another rough cloth. Strutt mentions the sarciatus, a garment of woolen cloth of inferior quality worn by the poor.

Startups were high "shooes" worn by rustics, called also bagging-shoes and peros (evidently a style existing since the Roman invasion). An old poem describes peasants' shoes or buskins as laced up in front, with soles full of wooden pegs.

HENRY III, 1216-1272

Materials.—The returning crusaders brought back many oriental fabrics.

Baudekin, called also ciclatoun, checklatoun, siglatoun and tissue, a sumptuous silk interwoven with gold thread, was believed to have originated in Babylon or Persia. It was of all colors and presented an embroidered appearance. Later it was called "brocat." Sarcinet was a thin silk.

Samite, a rich silk interwoven with gold, was brought to England during the reign of Richard, *Cœur de Lion;* when very lustrous it was called satin. Tinsel or tinsen were varieties of it. During the Middle Ages satin was usually colored red. Gazzatum was gauze. Gowns and mantles of silk were imported from Italy. Fur was lavishly used as lining, also for cloaks, borders and hats. A poem of the time alludes to "damask, velvet, purple pall, ermine and diaper." (This last is a much disputed term, some holding that it means embroidery on a rich ground such as cloth of gold; others, an all-over diamond design. Certainly the expression "diapered" so often encountered in old inventories and the like, would point to a recurrent pattern as the correct meaning.)

With all these magnificent materials placed at the disposal of the rich, no wonder men and women, perhaps with an eager desire to be clothed in all of them at once, went weighted down with yards and yards of material suspended from their shoulders. The age was therefore known as that of draperies.

The first armorial emblazoning on a surcoat is recorded in 1266; the heraldic age, however, was not well established until a hundred years later.

Footgear.—The points extended two inches beyond the toes and were whimsical as to direction, sometimes running straight in advance of the big toe, occasionally thrusting forward from the middle toe, but most frequently curling outward with a wriggly, serpentine suggestion. The boots were richly ornamented with gold stripes, also bands

of leather, cloth and rich materials. A V-shaped opening each side of ankle shoes facilitated dressing by dis-
pensing with fastening.

EDWARD I, 1272-1307

MEN

The hair was worn long and bushy.

WOMEN

The Kirtle.—A garment closely fitting the figure was
often laced, with long tight sleeves buttoned from elbow
to wrist. Over it was a loose gown of another color,
trained, with hanging sleeves often of considerable length,
lined to match the kirtle; the latter was allowed to show
in front by placing a girdle low on the hips and pulling
the overgown up through it. This gown was in universal
use for a long while and is invaluable in its effectiveness
for stage wear. The gorget accompanied it. (See the
French, thirteenth century, page 100, for description.)

The Spanish Turban.—The chin band and wimple
(dyed saffron) remained in fashion for older women,
with an endless variety of caps, one being the Spanish
turban. In this the forehead band became wide and stiff,
with one end of the gorget drawn up under it and allowed
to fall over the ear.

William Wallace, who lived in Scotland during this
period, should be costumed in late thirteenth-century
fashion.

CHAPTER XVII

THE FOURTEENTH CENTURY

HE Cote-Hardie.—This fashion originated in France and was universally adopted at the beginning of the fourteenth century. By shortening the surcoat, sewing up its sides and slitting open and closing the front with buttons, a tightly fitted jacket with long set-in sleeves was evolved. The latter were fastened by rows of closely set buttons from elbow to wrist. Fur (often ermine) was used to border it. It was worn by both men and women.

THE ITALIANS

The Lappet.—A band of fur, velvet or material different from the rest of the costume, was fastened on the sleeve of the cote-hardie above the elbow, with a long pointed piece of the same material depending therefrom. This was a distinguishing style note of the century and a souvenir of the trailing sleeve of former days.

Tights.—The cloth that had been held to the leg by cross-gartering, became known in the ninth century as tights, the materials being frieze and homespun. Cross-gartering was retained until the thirteenth century. Silk tights were common in Italy and Spain long before they became so in England during the reign of Elizabeth. These leg coverings were sometimes made with leather soles attached to the footpiece and worn without shoes, which accounts for the unshod look so noticeable in some very old pictures. In this century Italy had progressed to the point of having tights not only of silk but often embroidered in gold.

The Baselard.—A triangular pouch was suspended from the girdle, through which was thrust a dagger; it was of ornamental design and placed in front of the figure. In the fourteenth and fifteenth centuries its use was forbidden to priests.

The Chaperon.—A head covering popular among older men was achieved by using the hood with its liripipe (see the English, fourteenth century, p. 116) and cape. The head was thrust into the pocket of the hood usually filled up by the face. The cape was gathered into a huge rosette, its foliated edges lending themselves admirably to the purpose, and held to one side of this improvised hat by knotting around it the liripipe, whose long end was thrown about the shoulders like a scarf.

A cap, round and brimless, upstanding like a fez, was the favorite head covering of the youths of the day. By the end of the century a single feather, usually an ostrich plume of prodigious size, was placed in the front of the chaperon or cap. Hoods with shoulder capes were also worn. A portrait of Dante painted about 1300 shows him in a hood with a liripipe reaching to his waist.

Shoes were of velvet and leather, long and pointed.

Young men were clean shaven, with hair curled about the neck and brow. Older men wore beards.

The Houppelande.—Introduced in France during the century (for full description see the French, fourteenth century, p. 111), it was essentially a garment for the sedate and those of dignified position. Owing to its intro-

PLATE XIII. HEADDRESSES

A. Arrangement of blonde hair for Ophelia as worn by Ethel Barrymore (drawing after a photograph by White).

B. The caul worn by Lillian Gish as Romola (drawing after a photograph by Albin).

C. The caul as worn in England during the reign of Edward I (from a Royal MS.).

D. Veil and fillet as worn by Constance Collier as the Queen in "Hamlet."

duction the borders of costumes were foliated, scalloped or dagged. (See the English, fourteenth century, p. 116.)

WOMEN

The Simarre.—A gown of Florentine origin very popular among the women of Italy fitted the uncorseted figure closely to the hips where it widened into a full trained skirt. The sleeves were either very long and tight, terminating in a point over the back of the hand, or else elbow length with pendant lappet and a kirtle sleeve tightly buttoned covering the forearm from elbow to wrist. The simarre was also cut with long straight fronts, caught together at the neck line by a jewel, dividing thence to show a tight-fitting underdress.

The Crespine.—A caul of golden network was worn on the flowing hair. Garlands of flowers, golden bands and ribbon fillets were also used. Toward the end of the century small heart-shaped headdresses with lace wimples falling on each side began to be seen.

The period for "Romeo and Juliet" is the commencement of the fourteenth century; for the older characters such as Montague, Capulet and the Prince, a little theatrical license is allowed and they appear in the houppelande and chaperon, the latter even decorated with a plume, albeit these were fashions which came a bit later. All Romeos and Mercutios wear caps with long feathers trailing over the left shoulder. For them the cote-hardie, tights and velvet shoes with pointed toes are correct. The cote-hardie either buttons well up to the throat or is made with a square-cut neck opening filled in with a gathered shirt; Rollo Peters wore one with a deep round neck line about the shoulders, a pleated shirt edged with a flat band circling an inch or so above it.

The Drape.—Almost indispensable to all plays of the fourteenth and fifteenth centuries in which young men wear the cote-hardie and tights is the drape. It is a long piece of goods with a single hole through which the left arm is passed; this leaves a long end of the material which may be disposed of in various ways—as, for instance, gathered up from the floor and thrown across the chest and left shoulder, or pulled through the belt and allowed to hang again. Another trick is to wind the material over the right arm. Allowing it to trail on the ground after the wearer is an arrangement which, while sounding simple enough, requires careful rehearsal to insure adept handling. Lined with a bright color and cleverly managed, this wrap lends much charm to the actor's ensemble.

Of course, all Juliets wear the caul, that cap of criss-crossed pearls. Wreaths of flowers are also used to crown their flowing hair. The simarre appears in varied forms; Julia Marlowe pinned a "large gr-r-een jewel" on the front of hers for the first act. Jane Cowl's sleeves spread to huge wings trailing to the floor, exaggerated but attractive lappets. For the balcony scene the loose gown should be of some very sheer material of a shade that will seem a soft white with the spots playing on it; it should be made with very long, wide sleeves and a low girdle about the hips.

THE FRENCH

MEN

The Houppelande.—This long outer garment became the rage shortly after its introduction. It was worn over the cote-hardie and tights and buttoned from the high collar to the knees, whence it swept backward, often training on the floor. The sleeves were exceedingly wide from the elbows down and sometimes trailed on the ground, with foliated edges folded back upon the wrist for several inches, the better to show lining of a contrasting color, also the tight fitting sleeves of the cote-hardie beneath. The collar when left standing rose up over the chin; it was therefore left unbuttoned for two holes and turned over. For stage use the collar, rising and curving outward like a de Médicis, is sometimes attached to a yoke, both being made of the same material as the colored lining in the sleeves, the whole fitted to the rounded neck of the houppelande. This style was used with good effect in the Players' production of "Henry IV."

A shortened form of the houppelande was affected by young men, in which the skirt ended about the hips, allowing the legs to show.

The cote-hardie and tights, either parti-colored (see the English, fourteenth century, p. 115) or plain, were worn. The chaperon was very fashionable, also surcoats bordered with fur.

Poulaines (see the English, fourteenth century, p. 120).—Long-toed clogs were imported from Poland about the middle of the century. The anelace, a dagger, was stuck in the girdle and the gipcière worn with it. (See the English, Richard II, p. 120.)

The Pourpoint.—This was a stuffed and quilted doublet worn under or without armor, corresponding to the gambeson, panzar, etc.

After the battle of Crécy in 1346 cannon and rifles were

PLATE XIV. COSTUMES OF THE THIRTEENTH AND FOURTEENTH
CENTURIES

A, B, E and F. Varieties of the surcoat in 1200.
C and D. The kirtle gown and gorget and the age of draperies.
G. A particolored costume in the fourteenth century.
H and I. The houppelande and a Frenchwoman in a cote-hardie.

used; Chinese gunpowder had been made adaptable to fire-arms.

WOMEN

The cote-hardie, cut with a round low neck and richly trimmed with ermine, was worn with a full skirt caught up in front to show another of a different color. A jeweled girdle encircled the cote-hardie, whose long tight sleeves had lappets of ermine.

By the end of the century, heart and steeple headdresses, accompanied by the huge hennin, had made their début.

THE GERMANS

MEN

The cote-hardie was worn, and about either arm a lappet from which descended a cascade of gold tassels, each suspended from the one immediately above. Tights were without cross-gartering, and the whole costume parti-colored. Belts had fancy buckles. Hooded shoulder capes were worn. A knee-length tunic was in use with wide sleeves, the ends of which were long enough to tuck up through the belt.

Long hair was bound with gold bands, wreaths of gold, silver, etc. Leather skull caps were worn under helmets.

Low shoes, the leather decorated in an all-over diamond pattern, were in fashion. Gloves were worn by both men and women.

WOMEN

The women wore the same lappet as that described for the men.

The chin and mouth were almost covered by a wimple

edged with lace; this also received elaborate embroidery and was a forerunner of the ugly "barbe."

Sleeves of the outer gown, a form of the simarre, were often slashed open to the elbow and allowed to hang loose the length of the arm, the kirtle sleeve showing below the elbow. A bag and a bunch of keys hung from the waist.

The uncovered hair was arranged in a bang, then parted, braided and coiled about each ear.

THE ENGLISH: EDWARD II, 1307-1327; EDWARD III, 1327-1377

A period alluded to as "the Parti-Colored."

At this time a suit of full plate armor included the following pieces: The helmet visor (called the beaver when lowered), mentonnière (chin piece), neckguards, gorget, cuirass (or breastplate), back plate of cuirass, lance-rest, girdle, pauldrons (shoulder pieces), passegardes, rivets, palettes (armpit guards), brassards (upper arm guards), vambraces (lower arm guards), elbow pieces, gauntlets (mailed gloves), great braquette (waist pieces covering abdomen), tassets and tuiles (upper thigh guards), bracconière (mailed apron), gardes reines (loin guards), culet, cuishes (thigh guards), genouillières (knee pieces), greaves (or jambes), sollerets or pedieux (shoes of mail).

Mail armor was used in ancient and medieval days until the year 1300; it was followed by full plate and later leather (the latter sometimes in conjunction with plate). Fine specimens of old armor are to be found in the Wallace Collection and at the Tower of London.

MEN

Parti-Colored.—The cote-hardie and tights were parti-colored, that is, half the body was dressed in one color, the other half in another; frequently both colors appeared in stripes on one leg. The cote-hardie, always belted at the waist, where a pouch containing a dagger dangled, was of various lengths; a lappet hung from the arm. Long and short capes edged and collared with fur were buttoned at the neck.

The Dagged Fashion.—This (also known as foliated) appeared on all garments in 1346 and was promptly condemned by the clergy. These "dagges" were made by cutting away the material of the garment to form leaves, etc., about its edges.

The Liripipe.—The peak of the hood grew so long that it hung to the floor, requiring knots to be tied in it. This appendage became known as the "liripipe" and was often wound about the head with the end tucked in, or draped across the shoulders.

In 1319 the first placing of a plume on a helmet is recorded. Fur brims were used on hats. The toes of shoes increased in length and pointed outward; they were decorated in elaborate designs and showed rich contrast of color.

The Hair.—The hair was bushy, cut round and curled, the face clean shaven, although Edward II had a beard arranged in three curls. That of Edward III was very long. Old men wore their beards forked.

WOMEN

A full gown, sometimes trained, fitted the figure and was worn over a kirtle. Wide elbow sleeves hung over the tight ones of the inner dress. The cyclas, a tight-fitting surcoat, popular in the reign of Edward II, was shorter in front than behind.

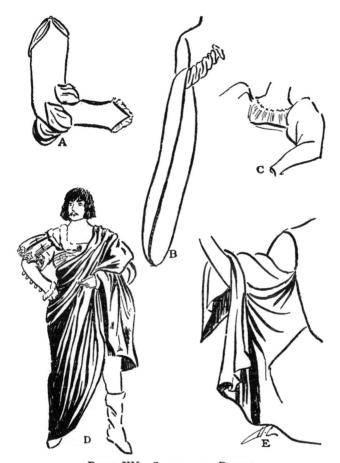

PLATE XV. SLEEVES AND DRAPES

A. Sleeve of a simarre worn by Mary Anderson as Juliet.

B. Sleeve with long lappets worn by Jane Cowl.

C. Sleeve as worn by Rollo Peters as Romeo.

D. The drape as worn by Lionel Barrymore in "The Jest" (sketched from a photograph by Abbé).

E. Drape brought under the arm and thrown outward.

Hairdressing.—Early in the century the gorget and the wimple, made of a fine cobweb lawn known as crisp, were in use. Young girls arranged the hair in two braids, one each side of the face, with the gorget laid under them and pinned behind; a fillet about the brow bound a wimple, which was sometimes placed like a veil over the gorget and braids. Silk ribbons in imitation of gold bands were called "bends" during the Middle Ages. The fashion of the two braids led to the adoption of cases of gold fretwork studded with jewels worn on either side of the face. The hair divided in two sections was drawn through them. The top of the head was left bare or covered by a wimple held by a fillet about the brow.

THE ORDER OF THE GARTER

In 1348 Edward III established this order; the costume consisted of a mantle, tunic and hood all of blue woolen cloth; the mantle was lined with scarlet and had one large garter embroidered on the left shoulder. It enclosed a shield argent charged with the cross of Saint George, gules. The tunic of the King was lined with ermine, that of a knight with minniver; both tunic and capuchon were thickly embroidered with small garters of blue and gold bearing the motto, *"Honi soit qui mal y pense."* The robe of the King displayed one hundred and sixty-eight garters.

The colors of the costume varied and its cut conformed to the prevailing fashion of the day for several centuries. During the pestilence in 1360, black was used as a sign of humility. Later came "sanguine ingrain" (purple). The garter, which was worn around the left knee, was made of blue cloth or of silk embroidered with gold, its buckles and chape of silver gilt.

SUMPTUARY LAWS, 1363

From time to time England enacted laws to regulate expenditure in the matter of clothes. At this date we find "Furs of ermine and lettice and embellishment of pearls, excepting for a headdress, strictly forbidden to any one not of the Royal family or a noble having upwards of 1,000 pounds per annum." Cloths of gold and silver, habits embroidered with jewelry, lined with pure minniver and other expensive furs, were permitted to knights and ladies whose incomes exceeded four hundred marks yearly. Knights whose incomes exceeded two hundred marks, or squires possessing two hundred pounds in lands or tenements, were permitted to wear cloth of silver, with ribands, girdles, etc., reasonably embellished with silver and woolen cloth of the value of six marks the whole piece; but all persons under the rank of knighthood or of less property than the last mentioned were confined to the use of cloth not exceeding four marks the whole piece, and prohibited from wearing silks and embroidered garments of any sort, or embellishing their apparel with any kind of ornaments of gold, silver or jewelry. "Rings, buckles, ouches (pins), girdles and ribands all forbidden decorations to them"; the penalty annexed to the infringement of this statute was "the forfeiture of the dress or ornament so made or worn."

RICHARD II, 1377-1399

The heraldic age commenced.

MEN

The Tabard.—A surcoat embroidered with the coat of arms of the wearer became an established fashion.

The chaperon was worn, or a cap decorated with a single ostrich plume in front. The cote-hardie, embroidered with precious stones and foliated, also tights were fashionable.

The houppelande (see the French, p. 111) became popular; it was worn very short by young men, the skirt being merely a ruffle below the waist.

The Baldrick.—A belt passing over the right shoulder carried the sword on the left hip.

Cloaks fastened on the right shoulder. Wide gold chains encircled the shoulders, either over the cote-hardie or the houppelande, from which hung ornaments or charms.

The Gipcière.—A pouch of stamped leather or velvet was attached by two straps to the waist; the dagger was sometimes thrust through it.

Cracowes (the Poulaines of the French).—These contraptions were introduced into England in 1384 and named for Cracow, Poland, where they were first used. A wooden sole, raised under the toes and ball of the foot with a pointed projection in front, intended to support the extremely long toe of the shoe, was held on by straps across the instep after the fashion of a modern skate. From 1390 on pattens with iron soles were used to raise the foot from the ground. The toes of shoes were stuffed or allowed to flop. Some were held to the knee by chains of silver or silver gilt. Garters were worn over tights below the knee.

The Hair.—Stained yellow with saffron, the hair was long and bound about the brow by bands of gold ornamented with enameled flowers. Mustaches were fashionable; older men wore beards trimmed to two points. Chaucer mentions forked beards. Richard II had a small mustache and two small tufts on the edge of his chin.

Jewelry was worn in abundance; despite sumptuary laws this was a time of great extravagance in dress. Feathers were placed on tournament helmets. Plate armor was in use.

WOMEN

Their dresses were very rich in material and ornamentation. There were no restrictions regarding crowns; all people of rank wore them. The cote-hardie, houppelande, fur-lined surcoat, a full trailing skirt and a cloak held across the chest by cords secured to the backs of large ornaments, were all in a woman's wardrobe. Her gown at this time has been called a "courtepy," also a kirtle and (by Chaucer) a "cote."

The Dorelet.—A caul made of gold net worn with all the hair tucked under it was called a dorelet. The back of the neck was shaved and the eyebrows plucked out; which two facts should convince the modern flapper that there is nothing new under the sun.

Long hair was bound with fillets or wreaths of flowers about the brow; wimples were used but the gorget was seen only on country women.

The Order of the Garter.—In 1384, violet ingrain was

used for the tunic; about 1388 white was substituted, but the original color, blue, became reëstablished the following year.

Famous people of dramatic or romantic interest during the century were: Philippa of Hainault, Queen of Edward III; Prince of Wales, called the Black Prince from the color of his armor; Robert Bruce, King of Scotland, 1306; Dick Whittington, 1358-1423; Geoffrey Chaucer; Gower; and Wat Tyler, a blacksmith.

The Theatre.—During the thirteenth and fourteenth centuries dramatic entertainment took the form of miracle plays and mysteries. The actors, numbering fourteen, were supplied with masks and tunics, the latter being made with hooded capes. The collection of masks comprised fourteen faces of women, fourteen bearded men, fourteen angels (silver), and twenty-eight fantastic heads representing animals. The tunics, each set numbering fourteen, were made of variously colored buckram and linen embroidered and painted, the decorations consisting of dragons' heads, peacocks' eyes, gold and silver stars and heads with wings. These frequently appeared on the front of the cape. See the pictures in the Bodleian MSS.

Materials.—Cloth of Tars, of disputed origin, probably came from Tartary. This expensive stuff was added to the constantly swelling list of costly goods from which, during the reign of Edward III, the rich might fashion their apparel. Cloth of gold, an eastern fabric of silk threads crossed by others of gold, made its appearance in the extravagant days of Richard II. Chaucer, to whom we are indebted for many tidbits regarding clothes, speaks of cendal (also called sendall, sandal and cindatum) as a thin silk; rash was a cheap variety; chaisel, for fine undergarments; chalon (Chaucer), a cloth garment "frysed" on both sides; falding, like frieze and used for bed covering (also a coarse red woolen cloth worn by Irish peasants); serge, mentioned by Chaucer but probaby in existence since the earliest coarse woolens; raynes (Chaucer), a name for bed sheets and shirts; volupere, a woman's cap; fustian, manufactured at Norwich in 1336, very strong woolen stuff used for jackets and doublets; buffin, a coarse cloth; bise, the skin of the hind used for fur; budge, lambskin with the wool dressed out, the ordinary fur trimming on citizens' robes; partlet, a gorget or rail on an old woman; frounce, a flounce; smocks (Chaucer); caul, named also a fret.

By an order of 1382 women of bad repute were obliged to wear hoods of ray only (striped Flanders cloth), and no budge (fur trimming), perreie (jewelry) or revers (facings).

CHAPTER XVIII

THE FIFTEENTH CENTURY

THE ITALIANS

ATE in the century a vast array of portraits by Titian, Leonardo da Vinci, Raphael and other painters guide us to the prevailing fashions of the time.

During the first half of the century young men wore tights and the cote-hardie, surcoats edged with fur, belts, pointed shoes and wide-sleeved houppelandes. Their hair was long and curled. In Venice, the hose began to offer the first suggestion of the pantaloon.

In the second half, the broad-shouldered, knee-length cloak with hanging sleeves bordered and heavily collared with fur, known as the petti-cote was worn over a tunic, at the top of which a circular necked, pleated shirt was visible; on the head was placed a round crowned hat with its brim upturned and cut in squares. The shoes had wide toes. Christopher Columbus was thus attired.

WOMEN

Early in the century a form of simarre was cut open on the sides and sleeveless, one jewel catching it together on the bosom; below showed the undergown. The sleeve of the latter was puffed at the elbow; small puffs were laid about the armhole extending down the back seam to the wrist. With it was worn the caul in many varieties.

PLATE XVI. FIFTEENTH-CENTURY HEADDRESSES

A. Headdress, France, end of the fourteenth century.
B. Horns draped by a wimple, England, Henry V.
C. The hennin tilted backward, reign of Richard III.
D. A fanciful steeple with gauze brim, reign of Edward IV.
E. The steeple with frontlet, reign of Edward IV.

Later on gowns were made with round or square low necks. The material of the dress was gathered to a fine embroidered band; above it showed a chemisette of fine linen or lace, its edge delicately outlined in black or gold. An enormous elbow-length sleeve had its wide end turned back as a cuff, the lower arm covered by an undersleeve of lace or linen caught to the wrist by a ruffled band. Sometimes a dark inner sleeve, made much too long, was pushed back in tiny folds as in the Mona Lisa. A full white underbodice was frequently worn, its upper edge showing above a velvet waist cut with a very low round neck. The mantles were voluminous, trimmed with broad fur collars.

The hair was parted in the middle and hung in curves or waves over the shoulders; crespines (cauls), jeweled fillets, wreaths, veils and the like adorned it. The portrait of Beatrice d'Este by Leonardo da Vinci which hangs in the Brera at Milan shows a golden crespine.

Ladies carried handkerchiefs.

THE FRENCH
MEN

The Roundlet.—This hat made in imitation of the chaperon was worn with the fur-edged, fur-collared houppelande, which dragged in a train. It had an upturned, stiffened brim on one side of which was fastened a cockade; a long streamer depended and was thrown carelessly about the shoulders.

A very tall brimless hat, also a cap with upturned brim and a long feather in front or hanging from the side, appeared. Enormous plumes decorated helmets throughout this century, and also the sixteenth.

When the houppelande was made with only a short frill

PLATE XVII. FIFTEENTH-CENTURY ACCESSORIES

A. The roundlet.

B. Sleeve, reign of Henry IV.

C, D and E. Shoes; England, fifteenth century.

F. French shoe; middle of the fifteenth century.

G. A queen of France wearing a heart headdress. The houppe-lande sleeves are lined with ermine. (From an old MS.)

H. The houppelande with foliated edges on sleeves.

below the waist, enormous sleeves were set in at the shoulder. Almost the whole of the tights showed.

Long-toed shoes and poulaines (cracowes, see the English, fourteenth century, p. 120) were used all the early part of the century; a shorter-toed variety was known as "poulaine de varlet."

In the latter half of the century, sleeves hung to the knees; in them were slits through which emerged the arm, covered with a tight inner sleeve of another color. Much brocade was used. The skirts of the cote-hardie were cut full and stiffened, reaching to the knees, the edges bordered with fur.

Tight boots to above the knee had lacings on the sides from ankle-bone to calf. Some had crosswise slits below the knees to give freedom of movement. Ankle-high shoes had turned back, pointed flaps on each side reaching to the sole. With the petti-cote, came square toes as in other countries.

WOMEN

The hennins, also the heart and steeple headdresses, were worn with the charming cote-hardie, a short-waisted, long-trained gown following, whose low-cut shoulders were edged by a broad band of material running to a crossed V at the waist line in front, its huge winged sleeves reaching the floor and showing a lining of fur. Toward the end of the century these great sleeves were turned back over the forearm. A hood of black velvet replaced the high headdress.

"As You Like It" is timed during the reign of Louis XII, in 1498. Touchstone wears a parti-colored tunic and tights, a hood with two peaks or ears, carries a bauble or folly stick in his hand while bells trim the costume at all points.

Jeanne d'Arc, born in France in 1412, dresses in plate armor of the period. Winifred Lenihan as Saint Joan wore a full cloth skirt gathered about the waist, a dark, sleeveless, low cut bodice of cloth closing up the front (not laced); a plain round-necked shirt with elbow sleeves.

An outstanding figure of dramatic and romantic interest was Chevalier Bayard, born in 1477 and dubbed "sans peur et sans reproche." He should be costumed in late fifteenth-century attire.

The kings of France were: Charles VI, 1380-1422; Charles VII, 1422-1461; Louis XI, 1461-1483; Charles VIII, 1483-1498. Louis XI dressed in shabby, patched clothes and wore a dilapidated felt hat; his courtiers disported themselves in the richest brocades, velvets and cloth of gold.

THE SPANISH

Silk, also a woolen fabric called "Spanish cloth," was manufactured. Tiraz was the name given a handsome silken material interwoven with inscriptions, names, etc. Spain and Portugal were both famous for woolen products.

MEN

The costume resembled the French. Some hats had wide rolled brims like turbans, a Moorish note.

WOMEN

The hair was arranged to give the impression of great length. This was accomplished by covering the whole

pendant braid by a veiling of gold webbing caught together in puffs at regular intervals, and extending below
the actual length of the hair.   White veils were also in use.

Sleeves were very large and puffed below the elbow.   A
tight-fitting bodice had a round neck; above it a full white
linen chemise was gathered to a band.   A full skirt was
worn.   A large mantle of brocade was made with slits
through which the arms were passed.   Spanish shawls
were embroidered and fringed.

The opera of "Il Trovatore" is laid in Aragon and Bis-
cay in the fifteenth century.

THE GERMANS

MEN

The class corresponding to the troubadours during the
first half of the century wore a cote-hardie laced up the
front with full sleeves gathered to an opening at the elbow.
From there a long round end with a foliated edge fell to
the knee.   A full, white undersleeve emerging at the elbow
covered the forearm to the wrist.   These sleeves were
typical of the period in Germany.   The cote-hardie and
the tights were parti-colored.   Their caps were trimmed
with foliated tabs on each side, some crowns resembling
bunches of leaves.

Hoods were made with knee-length capes, slashed up
the sides and rounded so that the arms could be used with
freedom, or carried beneath the folds.   Large hats of
fur were placed over the hood.   Surcoats had fur edging.
Ankle shoes were worn.

PLATE XVIII. COSTUMES OF THE FIFTEENTH CENTURY

A and D. Frenchmen, early and late in the century.
B. A form of the Italian simarre, a caul on the hair.
C. The roundlet and the cote-hardie, France and Spain, 1450.
E and F. The reign of Edward IV; clogs and the steeple head-dress.

WOMEN

There was a great variety in headdresses, especially during the second part of the century. Very heavy braids rested on the shoulders; a stuffed band covered with gold webbing, silk ribbon and jewels, was placed about the forehead; at the center, directly over the middle of the brow, was planted a small bow; a chin band was carried up over the roll and then placed under it at the back of the head with two long ends crossing and lying on the shoulders.

A headdress like the rolled pompadour of the Byzantine women had a wimple fastened by a brooch to its center.

A rolled turban, reminiscent of the Orient, with long folds brought through and hanging each side of the face, had cascades of gold tassels corresponding to the strings of pearls worn by the Byzantine women. The top of the turban was of a different color.

Another turban had a high gathered crown with a gold band jeweled at the center about the brow; over it was draped a white wimple. The edges of the wimple were embroidered and set over a stiffened forehead band. A few heart-shaped headdresses were used. For full dress, a high affair somewhat resembling the hennin and topped with plumes was worn.

At home a noble woman removed the fancy head covering and wore a white cap very like a Quaker bonnet.

Later in the century a round topped headdress, covered with gold webbing having two flaps of the same material at each side of the face, and finished with a black velvet forehead band, rose like a great orange. This was the largest headdress worn in Germany.

Elderly women used a cap with a rolled band; a jewel was placed at one side and a fold of linen descended to the left shoulder; they also had the gorget and wimple.

The gown corresponded to that worn in Italy and France during the middle of the century. Broad bands of embroidery were used as borders; the sleeves were tight fitting except for puffs let in at the elbow. Some sleeves were cut wide and much too long, so that the hands could be carried in them.

The houppelandes were made with enormous sleeves whose wide ends were foliated in streamers almost a foot deep; one variety was long and tight fitting, finished with an accordion pleated frill which hung many inches below the hand and completely hid it.

With the houppelandes was worn a headdress with foliated edges surmounted by a cluster of black cock feathers.

THE ENGLISH: HENRY IV, 1399-1413

About the year 1400 Henry IV revived the sumptuary laws. No man unless of high estate was permitted to wear cloth of gold or cloth of velvet or crimson, large hanging sleeves open or closed, or gowns so long as to touch the ground; the use of ermine, lettice or marten was forbidden to all such. No one having less than two hundred pounds in goods and chattels, or twenty pounds per annum, could wear ornaments of gold and silver. It was also decreed that no man, no matter what his condition, should be permitted to wear a garment cut "or slashed into pieces in the form of rose leaves, letters and posies of various sorts under the penalty of forfeiting the garments, and causing the imprisonment of the tailor who made them."

From all accounts, these sumptuary laws regarding costume seem to have been treated with no more respect than the Eighteenth Amendment.

MEN

Dagged edges were used on wide turned-back cuffs. The foliated work was for two centuries called "cut work."

Parti-colored tights and long pointed shoes were worn.

The Hair.—Short hair and mustaches were in favor. Beards appeared on older men. Henry IV had a short chin beard resembling a Van Dyck but arranged in two out-turned curls.

WOMEN

Clothes were plainer than in the previous reign, the hair often being left unbound.

"The Merry Wives of Windsor" is dated in this reign. The costumes usually resemble those of the reign of Richard II. Chaucer describes that of a physician of the time as being of scarlet and well furred, "as such a one ought to be." He dresses another one in purple and light blue lined with taffeta and cendal.

In the recent production of "Henry IV" by the Players' Club, the king and various earls wore houppelandes mostly fashioned of gold and silver brocades with high-standing turned-over collars of red, pink, green, etc. The long and foliated wide sleeves were lined with the same colors.

Prince Hal disported himself in the rather old-fashioned cote-hardie and tights. His shoes were black with a short pointed toe, their tops turned back showing a facing of blue and silver to match his costume. The hat had a peaked brim in front. The gold armor worn by him in the last act was royal and stunning.

Hotspur wore a cote-hardie of gold and black brocade with huge puffed sleeves tapering to a tightly fitted forearm (a cut slightly in advance of the contemporary style), gold-colored tights and black shoes with turned-over gold-faced cuffs. Prince John wore a short houppelande with long wide sleeve-ends and tights.

The ladies displayed the regulation trained gowns with cauls, jeweled bands and hoods on the head. Dame Quickly's costume was comprised of a full skirt with a well fitted tan bodice, both garments banded with stripes of a deeper tan; a white cap on her head.

Otis Skinner as Falstaff was dressed in a red and tan cote-hardie, red tights, high tan boots with wide tops and a huge felt hat whose long, crazy feather swept across the front.

In the last act, surcoats in vivid heraldic designs were worn over the armor, which was mostly plate; some, however, was of mail.

HENRY V, 1413-1422

MEN

Houppelandes were worn over armor.

Turbans, also a huge cap fastened to a rolled brim with the crown falling over one ear, were ornamented with one large jewel.

No beards were seen save on old men, and mustaches rarely. The hair was cut short and shaved about the back and over the ears resembling a vulgar style of recent years.

The Horned Headdress.—This was the first of the enormous headdresses to be adopted in England. The horns, of wire covered with gold webbing, jewel-studded, were placed at either side of the head. They attained great length as the fashion gained in popularity. The effect was somewhat softened when a wimple of lace or fine silk was laid over the whole. In all of the large headdresses, the hair was completely hidden by a cap of gold webbing.

The "orange" was the caul inflated over a huge wire frame completely covering the ears and hair. It was edged with a jeweled band.

The cote-hardie was made with a wide band of fur, usually ermine, running from neckline to hips in front. A full-trained skirt completed this charming costume.

HENRY VI, 1422-1461

MEN

Tall hats had brims upturned and cut in squares; fur was also used as a brim and to edge the face-openings in hoods. These high hats were placed on top of hoods that ended in shoulder capes. A turban with a rolled brim had a curtain of the material falling across the back of the neck, suggesting the Arab. Roundlets were also worn. (See the French, fifteenth century, p. 126.)

The hair was still worn short above the ears and cropped about the neck.

The same general lines appeared in the costumes, which now were of very rich materials; velvets and brocades of beautiful design made in Italy had become quite common.

Shoes had shorter toes and were laced up the sides.

The War of the Roses began in 1455; the House of

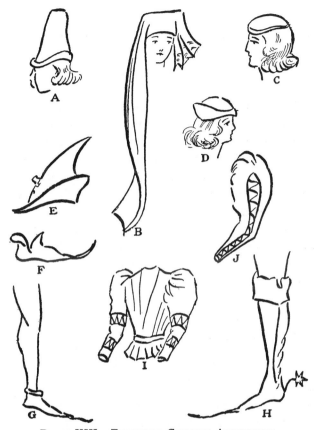

PLATE XIX. FIFTEENTH-CENTURY ACCESSORIES

A and E. Hats, England, Henry VI.
B. A form of the chaperon.
C and D. Small caps of black velvet, England, Edward IV.
F and G. Shoes, Henry VI.
H. Boot, Henry VI.
I and J. Form of trimming known as "hatched," Edward IV.

York was always represented by white roses; that of Lancaster by red.

WOMEN

The Heart-Shaped Headdress.—This was made by placing a padded roll in the form of a heart upon the head, with the curved ends over the brow. As in the "horned" much gold webbing, as well as jewels, appeared in the fabrication of this conceit. Wimples of linen, lace or silk covered the heart pad through the indented top and floated over the shoulders.

The gown during the middle of the century was cut low; a collar encircled the shoulders, crossed in front and disappeared into a high waistline. The sleeves, wide and long, were often turned back to the elbow. Trains were long and shoes pointed.

Plays dealing with Joan of Arc are dated in the reign of Henry VI of England.

EDWARD IV, 1461-1483

MEN

Footgear.—The length of the shoe was restricted by law to two inches beyond the toe. Failure to comply meant a fine of twenty shillings or a cursing by the clergy. This ruling must have been treated with open defiance, for clogs were in general use with a projecting support for the long toe, which was stuffed with moss or tow to stiffen it. Shoes reached to above the ankle, cut open on each side. High boots opened and laced down the entire length of the leg.

The hair was worn longer and bushy at the sides, with flat curls pasted to the forehead. Small round caps of

PLATE XX.   CHARLES JOHN KEAN AS RICHARD III

black velvet, skull-shaped, often adorned by a small feather on the side, were affected by young men.

In this reign tights showed almost to the waist.

The tunic opened wide in front; this and the full sleeves slashed open from shoulder to wrist were held together over the white shirt by gold lacings, drawn very tight to make the waistline small and the forearm slender. Such decoration was termed "hatched" and continued to the end of the next century. Another variety of tunic was allowed to hang loose to just below the waistline.

The tall hats of the previous reign were still seen. A long streamer of dagged ribbon was allowed to fall from the brim, a reminder of the old liripipe.

In the reign of Edward IV, only lords and their superiors could wear cloth of gold, purple silk, or sables; velvet, damask or figured satin was forbidden unless the income was one hundred pounds a year. Only lords might wear shoes with peaks more than two inches long, also the extremely short jackets. No yeoman was allowed to "stuff his doublet with wool or cotton." This must not cause confusion; the period of extreme padding occurred in the reign of Elizabeth. As the pictures in the reign of Edward IV show no eccentric form in the doublet, the foregoing is merely an allusion to the padding which tailors have always been wont to use in the sleeves of a man's coat.

WOMEN

The Steeple Headdress.—This was sometimes a yard high. A veil attached to its top floated down over the shoulders and train. The steeple was set back at an angle and finished with a velvet band around its lower edge; each side a flap of the velvet hung as low as the chin line, while a loop of the same material, known as the frontlet, was placed over the middle of the brow. The steeple was sometimes fashioned with a hanging brim of gauze held out by a wire very much like the transparent chiffon brims on modern hats.

Addison in *The Spectator* discourses on the steeple head-dress. The sumptuary laws of Edward IV permitted wives and daughters of men possessing the yearly value of ten pounds to use frontlets of black velvet or "of any other cloth or silk of the color of black." Princesses of the House of Tudor had frontlets of gold.

RICHARD III, 1483-1485; EDWARD V, 1485-1487

MEN

The tunic, reaching to the knees, was cut very full and arranged in box-pleats.

The Petti-cote (so called from the shortness of its skirts).—A broad-shouldered, knee-length cloak, fur-edged with an enormous collar of the same, began to make its appearance; at first, the long loose sleeves hung free from the elbow.

White shirts, elaborately pleated about their tops, rose to a low round neck line.

Shoes were no longer pointed but were gradually becoming wide and square across the toes, with very low sides somewhat resembling bedroom slippers.

Round crowned hats had upstanding brims cut out in squares or scallops and fastened up by jewels or buttons.

The hair was long and bushy; faces clean shaven.

WOMEN

The Hennin.—At first this headdress rose high in the air. Over a cap of gold webbing studded with gems, billows of the finest lawn, lace-trimmed, were held up by a wire frame set about the head. Gradually the shape spread backwards, like two great sails or wings. The hennin was popular on the Continent long before the craze for it attacked England.

HENRY VII, 1487-1509

As Henry of Richmond, he defeated Richard III at Bosworth Field in 1485, thus terminating the War of the Roses. By marrying Elizabeth of York he united the White Roses with the Red. This was the commencement of the Tudor Period.

MEN

The materials in use were very rich. The collar of fur became very deep and square at the back, running down in long revers to the waistline in front. Large coats reached to the ground. Sleeves fitted the shoulders but became very large and hung in folds on the forearms.

The petti-cote was now an established fashion; combined with a girdle and a handsome, often jeweled, stomacher, also called "placcard," lacing up the front.

Slashing (also called Blistering).—This became a craze and extended to all parts of the costume. The gallants of the day wore "bulwarks," a name given to their slashed and puffed knees, adopted in imitation of the Swiss soldiers. Slashes in the stomacher gave glimpses of the white shirt beneath.

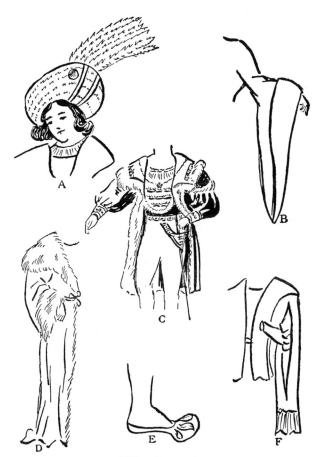

PLATE XXI. TUDOR ACCESSORIES

A. Feathered hat, England, Henry VII.

B. A woman's sleeve, England, Henry VII.

C. The petti-cote as worn in "The Firebrand," showing fur-trimmed placcard and gathered shirt.

D. Long cloak with fur collar and cuffs, England, Henry VII.

E. Broad shoes with slashed toes, Henry VII and Henry VIII.

F. Hanging sleeves on a petti-cote, Henry VII.

The low round neck of the preceding reign gave way to a high line ending in a neckband.

Striped tights were worn.

Broad-toed shoes of velvet or leather were slashed across the toes to allow a puffing of white or of a contrasting color to show. A sandal consisting of a flat sole with a covered toe piece was much worn; this was attached to the foot by a single leather strap across the instep.

The berretino was a round crowned hat with square-cut brim into which was stuck a feather. A high feathered bonnet was worn on one side of the head over a skull cap and fastened by a strap under the chin. Feathers were used in profusion.

The Order of the Garter.—In 1504 a decided change took place. Following the fashion of the time, a collar was put on the tunic, which was of purple velvet lined with white silk (sarcenet or taffeta). The embroidering of garters was discontinued.

WOMEN

A square-cut neck was filled in by a pleated white chemise, the gown fitting well with a long train attached. Sleeves were tight to the elbow, ending in a very broad hanging cuff which was often made of fur. Fur was also used as borders and lining for trains. These last were sometimes turned up and fastened to the waist in order to exhibit their elegance.

A tight-fitting cap of linen or colored material covered the hair. Over it was worn a baglike cap usually of black, which hung down over the shoulders. A wide stiffened band of material, embroidered or sewn with pearls, was n stop.

then bent in the center and placed over the hood so as to border the face and hang to the shoulders.

Black caps or hoods were very popular. These were slit at each side behind the ear; the front flap then turned or buttoned back on the main section, allowing the edge of a snug-fitting linen cap to show about the face. Cauls of gold wire in imitation of the German fashion were used at the end of this reign. For old ladies and widows, the barbe of pleated linen covering the lower face and chin was customary.

Materials.—Linsey-woolsey, a coarse woolen fabric; drugget, used for common clothing and resembling baise; dowlas, a linen used by the lower classes; canaber, a linen cloth of which hose were made; stamium, coarse worsted; tabby, a thick silk with a soft nap; champeyn, a fine cloth (reign of Henry VI); cadace, the name given stuffing of silk, cotton, wool and tow, were new materials used.

Christigrey was the name of a fur; mink was written "mynke." The broad-toed shoes were termed "duck-bills."

Famous people of dramatic interest during the fifteenth century were: William Caxton; Henry Tudor, Earl of Richmond; Stafford, Duke of Buckingham; Fox, Bishop of Winchester; Jean Gutenberg; Ferdinand and Isabella; Christopher Columbus; Sebastian Cabot; Jane Shore; Michaelangelo; Raphael; Dürer; Da Vinci; Botticelli; Fra Filippo Lippi; Pope Alexander VI.

The Theatre.—Moralities succeeded the miracle plays about the middle of the reign of Henry VI. At the close of the fifteenth century, mythological masques and "interludes" were popular forms of entertainment.

CHAPTER XIX

THE SIXTEENTH CENTURY

THE ITALIANS

MEN

ANY copied the short-waisted, knee-length German coat (see the Germans, sixteenth century, p. 151), with hanging sleeves. The stomacher or placcard was of a different color; above it a pleated shirt, low necked and edged with a tiny ruffle. Others wore a doublet with large puffed sleeves and slashed hose over which were worn, both above and below the knee, garters of silk and gold. A shoulder cape with a high standing collar was popular. Broad-toed velvet shoes were worn.

The bragetto, a jeweled pouch, hung at the waist.

Mantles with large armholes through which the puffed sleeve of the doublet could be passed were sometimes made with loose hanging sleeves thrown back over the shoulders like drapery.

The hair was short. The hat known as the "Milan Bonnet" (see the Germans, sixteenth century, p. 150) was followed by one of black velvet peculiar to Spain (see the French, sixteenth century, p. 153).

WOMEN

The Virago Sleeves.—These sleeves, very large and slashed open from shoulder to wrist, giving glimpses

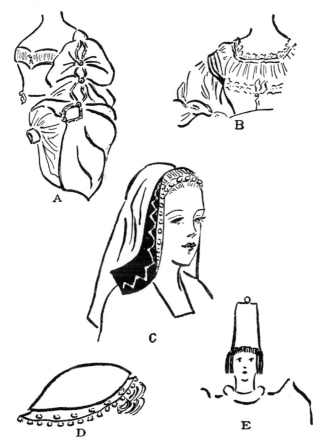

PLATE XXII. DETAILS OF COSTUME, CLOSE OF THE FIFTEENTH
CENTURY

A. Virago sleeve (detail from Raphael's portrait of Jeanne
d'Aragon).

B. Gathered chemisette (from Raphael's portrait of the Fornarina).

C. French hood (from the portrait of Suzanne de Bourbon, 1495).

D. The Milan bonnet; a form frequently used by Holbein. early
sixteenth century.

E. Tall hat, France, fifteenth century.

of rich lining, were caught together at intervals by jewels. Points, and a series of puffs, were used as trimming about the armhole. A full inner sleeve of white lawn or other material was gathered to a tiny wrist ruffle. Occasionally the outer sleeve was lengthened to reach the floor and hung free, or else was thrown back over the shoulders displaying a rich contrasting lining. This fashion soon spread to all countries.

Sleeves were also made in a series of puffs, very large at the shoulder and gradually diminishing in size as they neared the wrist. Slashing and jeweling appeared on the puffs.

Dresses were cut with the waist running down to a long point over the abdomen; the skirt very full and trained. Most of the gowns had a high standing collar across the shoulders, having its center point sometimes bent forward over the head; a fashion of Roman origin which quickly spread to Padua, Venice and France.

Venetian women wore veils suspended from the head and hanging to the feet, their corners sometimes caught up under the point of the bodice.

Turbans of cloth of gold were attached to a band or diadem set with precious stones.

The hair was drawn straight back from the brow, coiled and adorned with jeweled bands or ropes of pearls.

An early sixteenth-century portrait seen in the Poldi-Pezzoli Collection, Milan, shows a tiny cap of gauze fitted over the ear; to it is attached a string of pearls which connects with the rest of the headdress. Perhaps the lady had "cauliflower" ears, or it may have been a passing fad of the moment. The Milan bonnet was popular. Long neck chains were of gold with beautiful feathered, gold-

PLATE XXIII.   HEAD COVERINGS AND HATS, BEGINNING OF THE
SIXTEENTH CENTURY

A. Milan bonnet worn over a caul of cloth of gold.

B. The French hood (from a portrait in the Altman collection).

C. The French hood (as shown in a portrait of Catherine of
Aragon).

D. The gauze ear-cap (detail of a portrait in the Poldi-Pezzoli
Collection, Milan).

E. Milan bonnet over a caul of cloth of gold; earrings, late Henry
VIII.

handled fans attached; the Venetian fan was much used
Small ruffs appeared on some high-necked dresses.

"Two Gentlemen of Verona" takes place in Italy early
in the sixteenth century; "Much Ado about Nothing" is
of the same period, while "All's Well That Ends Well"
is dated 1557, the time of Cosimo de' Medici. Part of the
"Winter's Tale" is laid in Italy during the first half of
the century. Victor Hugo's tragedy of "Angelo" is
dated 1547 and "Lucrezia Borgia," 1500.

At this time the cardinals wore red cloaks with large
flat broad-brimmed hats whose hanging cords were knotted on the chest. A cape of ermine could be seen through
the cloak opening.

Prelates had long black gowns with lace tunics to the
hips and capes to the elbow, a large black cloak and a
skull cap of the same hue.

The dalmatica was a long, full-sleeved tunic in color,
fringed at the bottom and worn over a white one called
the alb. The latter had a band of embroidery across the
front at the feet. The chasuble was cone-shaped with a
hole just large enough to pass the head through, so that
the cloth fitted the shoulders smoothly; the sides were
gathered up in folds over the arms when the priest celebrated. This fullness was later cut away.

THE GERMANS

MEN

The petti-cote had hanging sleeves. Above it a very
high full shirt was gathered about the neck.

The Milan Bonnet.—This style, despite the name, is
said to have originated in Germany, and quickly spread

to Italy and other countries. A cap of cloth or velvet was worn cocked on one side of the head over a caul of cloth of gold; the edges of its brim were often slashed into square flaps which could be bent back and forth at will. The trimming consisted of a bunch of feathers ornamented with gold spangles and jewels, or a cluster of points or tags placed on one side.

Points (also called Tags).—Ribbons with metal tags attached formed a decoration which lasted for a couple of hundred years.

A large bag cap had a wide fur edge.

Low shoes with slashed square toes, also high ones, were cut in bent-back points about the top, thus displaying a colored lining.

Enormous coats had wide fur collars which completely covered the shoulders; revers of fur continued to the knees in front. The sleeves were either cut off at the wide armhole or continued in hanging affairs, with openings for the tunic-covered arm to pass through.

The soldiers were subjected to an enormous amount of "slashing" and presented a bewildering mass of color. This was particularly true of the Bavarian troops. Large hats had their brims cut in squares; great plumes in two different colors surmounted the crown. The legs were striped in different colors, perhaps one in red and white, the other yellow and red; the shoe on the first mentioned might be blue, that on the other, red. Large bows of ribbon, possibly blue, were placed at the knees. Besides red, blue and yellow, another color was worked into the doublet and shirt.

The soldiers' tights received a new touch which was adopted by the citizen: slashes (the French being blamed for starting the fashion) were cut at the knees and about the hips and the openings filled in with puffings of another color.

Helmets were decked with enormous plumes; the same decoration was used on the horses of the cavalry. Full plate armor was worn. A gold chain about the neck signified a badge of office throughout the century.

WOMEN

The gowns were very much as before, full trained, bordered and held up to show an undergown; the sleeves presented a series of puffs, with one, slashed, called a "mahoitre," hanging about the armhole. A high wired collar was placed about the neck. Wide borders and slashing were used unsparingly.

A very coarse gold caul studded with pearls was worn over the hair, which was braided and arranged to stand out from the head in a semicircle across the back.

Enormous hats, wide brimmed, covered with ostrich plumes and bound with two colors (an exaggerated form of the Milan bonnet) were set well back on the head over the caul.

The barbe of linen and various other materials, resembling a man's beard where it covered the face below the nose, was very fashionable. A cap like the Mary Stuart was popular during the middle of the century; also ruffs.

Men and women carried gloves in the left hand.

THE FRENCH

MEN

In the Musée d'Artillerie in the Invalides at Paris is a large collection of Italian, French and Bavarian armor of the sixteenth century.

Men wore the petti-cote and slashed tights; doublets and trunk-hose; doublets and French breeches; and ruffs so large that eating in a seemly manner was difficult.

The Milan bonnet was followed by a black velvet hat with a small stiff brim, its crown tapering to a peak.

Small Italian capes with high standing collars were suspended from the shoulders; there also appeared the collarless one of the Spaniards, accompanied by a ruff and the black velvet hat.

By the end of the century, the hair fell in lovelocks at one or both sides of the face.

The rabat was a neckband with flaps falling in front over the costume and was worn chiefly by French ecclesiastics.

WOMEN

For the first half of the century, a gown trailed on the floor all around with sleeves much puffed from shoulders to elbows, from whence they tapered to fit the wrists. The high neck was finished with a small ruff.

The French hood was of black silk early in the century. In the middle, when the black velvet hat, exactly like that of the men, was cocked on the head, the hair was pulled back from the forehead and dressed very high. The Mary Stuart cap was, of course, worn.

During the second half of the century came into fashion the farthingale (in French "vertugadin" and in old French "vertugade"—probably corrupted from "vertu-garde," which, translated, would mean virtue guard). The gown then was much slashed, carrying an enormous standing collar of lace stretched on wires. Catherine de' Medici insisted that all ladies of the court reduce their waists to a circumference of thirteen inches; accordingly, an instrument of torture made of wooden sticks was placed around the figure and tightened to such a degree that the ribs overlapped and the abdomen protruded. This corset was largely responsible for the stiffness and ugliness of the farthingale period.

Feather fans with mirrors set in the center, also the pomander (see the English, sixteenth century, p. 158) dangled from a chain about the waist. Handkerchiefs were carried in the hand.

THE SPANISH

The Spaniards of this time wore black velvet hats and shoulder capes, pointed beards, curled mustaches, close cut hair, handkerchiefs, silk stockings and virago sleeves. Earrings were affected by Spanish noblemen, and the picado, a flaring and enormous ruff, was worn in the sixteenth and seventeenth centuries.

Famous people of dramatic interest on the Continent were Rabelais, Montaigne, Rubens, Tintoretto, Titian, Romano, Ribera, Holbein, Del Sarto, El Greco, Veronese, Vos, Jan Brueghel, Benvenuto Cellini, Cervantes, Lope de Vega, Don Carlos (1545-1568, son of Philip II of Spain, a hero of tragedies by Schiller and Alfieri), Charles V (Emperor of Germany and Spain), Duke of Guise, Catherine de' Medici (responsible for the Massacre of

PLATE XXIV. SIXTEENTH-CENTURY COSTUMES

A. Italy, early in the century.
B and C. Henry VIII of England and a Frenchwoman.
D and E. A French couple, 1550.
F. A style common to Italy and Spain, 1550.

Saint Bartholomew, 1572), Francis I (King of France, 1515-1547), and Martin Luther.

The Theatre.—Early in the sixteenth century the drama had been greatly encouraged in Rome by Pope Leo X. Many traveling companies of Italian actors came to France, where a craze for dramatic productions had existed since early in the fifteenth century. Performances were commanded by Catherine de' Medici at Blois and Henry IV at Fountainebleau. The Italian players seem to have become an established mode, for several companies were in Paris at the end of the century.

THE ENGLISH: HENRY VIII, 1509-1547

MEN

Early in this reign the full, high-waisted coat reached nearly to the knees, with shoulders padded to a great width. Large sleeves were made of material matching the waistcoat or stomacher, the latter much slashed and showing through the open front of the coat. Sleeves were fashioned either in one with the petti-cote, or were integral garments that could be detached, so providing variety. The shirt, called by some the partlet, the baggy breeches and sleeves, were all slashed and puffed. The lining, visible through the slashes, was dubbed "pullingsout."

The shirt, displayed above the waistcoat and sometimes through its slashes, had a plain band of one or two inches in width placed above its neck by Henry VIII.

The slashing about the knees and hips of the Swiss soldiery led to separating the tights into two garments, *i.e.,* hose and breeches, or, in common parlance, the nether and upper stocks, respectively. A later designation was trunk-hose and trunks.

The Milan bonnet, trimmed with a profusion of feathers, was worn over a skull cap. Night caps of black velvet were used by the Tudors.

The flat-soled sandals of the previous reign were still popular; also the shoes, whose toes became so broad their width was restricted by proclamation to six inches.

The hair was long; that is, curled inward like a bob until 1521, when Henry ordered all his attendants and courtiers to "poll their heads." Beards and mustaches were worn.

A cane was carried by Henry VIII, its top serving as a receptacle for perfume or snuff. The King had a one-handed watch suspended about his neck. Minute hands did not exist until the seventeenth century.

The petti-cote gave way to the doublet, its high neck finished with a small ruffle; long sleeved, with a short skirt below its waistline, allowing the trunks to show. The trunks and sleeves were decorated with long slits or slashes.

The Order of the Garter.—A surcoat of crimson velvet was worn with a black Milan bonnet of the same material; the crimson velvet hood was thrown over the left shoulder. About 1521 Henry bestowed the great and the lesser George on the knights; this jewel was suspended from a gold chain upon the breast until late in the reign, when a black ribbon was substituted.

WOMEN

The square-cut bodice was laced tight, the sleeves fitting the arms for several inches below the shoulders, then widening to form a square cuff turned back to show an undersleeve of white. The gown was open in front, revealing an underskirt. Some skirts were cut round after a Dutch fashion worn by Anne of Cleves. The train of Catherine Parr, however, was two yards long.

The Pomander.—All waists were encircled by girdles from which dangled these trinkets, hollow balls filled with perfume. In various shapes, the fashion lasted throughout the sixteenth and seventeenth centuries.

The headdress retained the hood as in the previous reign, but its peaked effect gave place to a rounded front, held away from the forehead by a pad. Anne Boleyn wore a Milan bonnet; all of the King's other wives wore the hood with the exception of Anne of Cleves, who is represented in a caul. A bongrace was a frontlet placed on the hood to prevent sunburn; Anne Boleyn had one and this device was seen during the entire century.

During the eighth year of this reign it was ordained that "duchesses and countesses and all higher estates may be barbed above the chin, every one not being under the degree of a baroness may wear a barbe about the chin; and all other gentlewomen beneath the throat-goyll" (gullet).

Shakespeare's "Henry VIII" is dated 1521, at which time there were many laws governing the use of materials. All persons not possessing an income of two hundred marks a year were forbidden to wear velvet, marten fur, chains, bracelets or collars of gold. Their sons and heirs, however, might clothe themselves in black velvet or damask, tawny russet or camlet. It was necessary to have one hundred marks per annum to appear in satin and damask.

PLATE XXV. MIDDLE-CLASS COSTUMES, FIFTEENTH AND SIXTEENTH
CENTURIES

A. A fifteenth-century German.
B and C. An English couple, 1450.
D and E. German women in 1550 and in 1500.
F and G. An English couple, Tudor period.

Pleated shirts decorated with gold, silver or silk might be worn by knights. Any one of lesser degree than a baron or knight's son or heir, could not wear crimson or blue velvet, embroidered clothes or "garments bordered with gold sunken work."

The fur of the black jennet was for royal use alone, while only those above the rank of viscount could wear sables.

Beerbohm Tree as Cardinal Wolsey wore scarlet satin with a cap of black velvet. There is a famous portrait of Wolsey by Holbein. An inventory of the Cardinal's effects mentions clothes made of the following materials: velvet, satin, damask, taffeta, grosgrain, sarsenet and caffa (a rich East Indian stuff).

Other fabrics in use at the beginning of the sixteenth century which previously have not been mentioned were: camlet, wool and silk mixed, but originally of camel's hair; Russell's or Brighton nap, a black woolen cloth resembling baise but with knots scattered over its surface; grogram, woolen cloth like grosgrain; taffeta, a thin silk and a luxury.

"Branched" was a term applied to the very large patterns representing fruit, flowers and vines used on satin and brocade at the beginning of the Tudor period.

Bristol red, not so bright as scarlet, was a favorite color throughout the century.

The lower classes had cogware, a cloth like frieze; rug, coarse woolen stuff for the very poor; wadmoll, an inferior fabric; shanks, cheap fur trimming from legs of kids or sheep. Canvas shirts were worn. Damicaster was the name given a short cloak worn by women of the middle class. A flocket was a loose, wide-sleeved gown

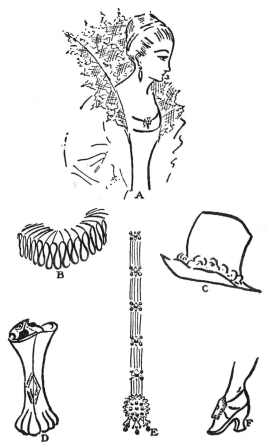

PLATE XXVI. DETAILS OF COSTUME, TIME OF ELIZABETH OF
ENGLAND

A. Lace collar as worn by Katherine Cornell in "Will Shakespeare"
(drawing after a photograph by White).

B. An Elizabethan ruff.

C. Hat (from a portrait of Francis Bacon).

D. The Venetian chopine, sixteenth century.

E. The pomander.

F. An Italian shoe, sixteenth century.

used by old women. Felt hats were worn. Russet clothes, of reddish brown or gray, were the ordinary garb of country people.

The Theatre.—During the sixteenth century, characters from the Bible were mixed up with the allegorical figures so popular in the earlier forms of the drama. Some attempt at costuming was made for Richard Gibson, an actor during the reign of Henry VII, writes about the dresses used for Venus and Beauty. An inventory dated 1516, time of Henry VIII, speaks of a long garment fashioned of cloth of gold and "tynsell," worn, by the actor playing a prophet on Palm Sunday.

EDWARD VI, 1547-1553; MARY ("BLOODY"; married Philip of Spain), 1553-1558

MEN

The doublet was in a stage of transition with the sleeves much smaller. A tiny ruff was introduced on it through Spanish influence, which also was responsible for the fashion of the short collarless shoulder cape reaching to a little below the waist.

WOMEN

The hair, with the exception of a small puffing at the sides, was well covered by the headdress known as the "Mary Stuart."

Mufflers (barbes) were worn for many years, and their use not confined to widows and old women by any means, for Anne Boleyn had one in her wardrobe. Mary, Queen of Scots, wore one fashioned of black satin in 1564 and Elizabeth in 1579 was presented with a barbe made of purple velvet "embroidered with Pearls and Venetian lace trimmed."

ELIZABETH, 1558–1603; THE ELIZABETHAN PERIOD

MEN

The Doublet.—Close fitting, with epaulets hanging over the armholes, the doublet was a jacket closed to the ruff; the waistline dipped to a deep point in front, while below a short ruffle or skirt extended to a depth of three or four inches. In time this ruffle was cut at regular intervals into a series of square tabs, giving a much trimmer look to the garment. The sleeves, if sewn in, were usually tight fitting; an epaulet, commonly known as a wing, puff-wing or welt, always finished off the armhole. When virago sleeves were worn, they were tied in with points (see the Germans, sixteenth century, p. 151), which gave the necessary trimming at the shoulder. Decoration in some form around the armhole lasted until coats came into fashion. The points or tags were also known as aiglets or aiguilettes and sometimes represented small figures, which explains why Grumio called them "aglet-babies." The doublet, usually of two thicknesses and wadded, was worn over corsets by the dandies. In 1583 its front was stuffed just above the waistline with four or five pounds of rags, tow or anything handy until it resembled the abdomen of Mr. Punch. These inflated affairs were called pease-cod-bellied, or shotten-bellied, doublets. They were often fashioned of the most expensive materials and much slashed.

The Jerkin.—Of leather, limited to eight tabs below the waistline, and sometimes confounded with the doublet over which it was often worn for extra protection, this garment was used by servants and workingmen; also by soldiers during the sixteenth and seventeenth centuries, when it was made of buff leather.

The Mandillion.—A loose coat, buttoned or open, was sometimes placed over a doublet; it had two broad wings over the shoulders, with hanging sleeves.

The Jornet.—This loose cloak was used for traveling.

Gally (or Gallic) Breeches.—Wide trunks were worn by every one early in the reign. They were made of broad bands of material running vertically, with a puffing of another color showing between suggesting stripes. Originally the hose was seen through slashes in the trunks. For stage use it is customary to make the trunks with alternate vertical bands of different materials as a closed separate garment. During eight years, ending in 1583, it was fashionable to pad or bombast these breeches to an enormous size with a stuffing of tow, rags, bran, etc.

French Breeches.—This variety of French hose, which became almost as popular in England as in France, fitted the leg tight to below the knee, where they were finished with canions, *i.e.,* rolls of material or puffing decorated with slashes.

Venetian Breeches.—Well fitting and finished below the knee with points, the material was covered with panes (diamond-shaped openings) which rendered a handsome lining visible. Gold laces and often jewel insets further added to the cost of this variety. Velvet, silk and damask were utilized.

For older men a long coat, tight fitting about the waist and retaining the long hanging sleeves of the petti-cote, was worn buttoned up the front or left open allowing the trunks to show.

Footgear.—Shoes were pointed in the toe and made of variously colored leather, velvet or "taffety"; white, black, red and green were popular. Early in the reign they were decorated with slashes, which often were studded with jewels. Later, ribbon roses on high-heeled low shoes were worn. Bottom, in "Midsummer Night's Dream," tells all of his fellow actors to buy new ribbon for their pumps. This form of shoe continued in use for servants, especially footmen, during the seventeenth century.

High leather boots reached to above the knee and were pricked in patterns; their tops were cut in squares to form a fancy edging; fur also was used for this purpose.

Hats.—Beaver, velvet and "taffety" were used for the rich and felt for the poor. With small curved brims and bell crowns, or flat and round, they were usually set off by a feather placed in front or to one side.

The Ruff.—At first merely a small ruching about the neck of a doublet, by 1582 the ruff had grown to a width of nine inches and was dubbed the "cartwheel." (The credit for introducing the ruff is given a certain princess who, living in sunny Spain, placed a ruffle about her neck to conceal a goiter.) Made of cambric and lawn, it was starched in different colors, blue, white, purple and yellow being fashionable. A craze for the last hue developed; even when a Mrs. Turner, wearing a yellow ruff, the preparation for the coloring of which she had invented, was hanged at Tyburn—though not for that reason!—it occasioned only a slight lapse in its popularity.

The Supportasse.—An arrangement of wires covered

with gold, silver or silk thread was worn around the neck to support the ruff. The pleat of a ruff was called a purl. Poking-sticks of wood or bone, and later of steel, were used to push out its crumpled folds.

The Piccadilly.—A high ruff edged with lace was named after the Spanish picado (in Old French "piccadille," which became in English "pickadil" and, finally, "piccadilly").

The Falling Band (or Rabato).—A plain white collar was sometimes composed of three sections laid one over another and attached to a linen band. Ben Jonson, the actor Burbage, Milton, Drake and many others are represented wearing it.

The Hair.—This was brushed back from the forehead and a bit over the ears when accompanied by the pointed beard. The dandies copied foreign modes, there being several to choose from: short, round and curled like the Italian's, long at the ears and curled like the Spanish, or French lovelocks tied with ribbons and lying on the shoulders. So much fuss was made over the hair that gentlemen carried pocket glasses.

After 1560 beards came again into favor and men were very particular about the cut. Of the many varieties, the pointed, the stiletto and the spade were the most popular. The pique-devant was a full beard trimmed to a fine point. Dyeing was fashionable; Bottom speaks of "straw-colored, orange-tawny, purple ingrain, French crown color and perfect yellow beards." Pasteboard cases were used to preserve their shape at night. Mustaches, called also mowchatowes and mouchaches, were worn in various styles; some brushed carefully up from the lip and

PLATE XXVII. ELIZABETHAN, STUART AND PURITAN COSTUMES

A and C. The stomacher and farthingale in France and England.
B. Man, time of Elizabeth.
D and E. A couple, reign of Charles I.
F and G. A Puritan couple.

curled, others drooping. Periwigs were in use. Faces were whitened with chalk.

Jewelry and Ornamentation.—Rings, chains about the shoulders, jewels in the hat, and earrings (a Spanish fashion), often in only one ear, were all worn. Earstrings resembling black shoe laces were tied through a hole in the ear. Portraits show, and old plays mention, them. In one of the latter a man is dragged out of a tavern brawl by his earstring. This freakish fashion was indulged in also by women. A rose stuck over the left ear was the badge of a lover.

In 1577 pocket watches were brought to England from Germany, but worn only by the wealthy.

The toothpick was a fashionable accessory.

Order of the Garter.—A high crowned hat was worn during this reign.

WOMEN

A well fitting bodice with a small ruff and long, hanging, winglike sleeves which reached the ground was attached to a full skirt early in the reign; this combination opened in front to show a contrasting color. The accompanying headdress was of the style known as Mary, Queen of Scots, with a long veil depending.

In 1583 the bodice was stuffed like the men's doublet.

Girdles of gold cord had pomanders attached; feather fans were set with mirrors.

The ill-fated beauty, Mary, Queen of Scots, wore a rich trained gown of silk and velvet at her execution; a long linen veil hung from her head.

The Farthingale.—In 1590 a huge bone wheel, suspended from the waist by ribbons, was used to swell the figure to enormous proportions about the hips. Over it were laid several stiff linen underskirts. A petticoat of heavy stuff such as brocade often embroidered in silver, and an overgown of some material affording a contrast in color, were then adjusted. The bodice of the latter fitted over a stomacher held in shape by the stiff straight line of the busk, *i.e.,* the carved wood corset of the time, compared with which the high Victorian affair that called down so much condemnation in the nineteenth century, must have been a downy nest. To help support the farthingale, padded rolls five inches long called "bearers" were placed at the back of the figure on each hip. A corset with stomacher and bearers attached is in the South Kensington Museum, London. The overgown opened down the front to display the petticoat, the material of which was duplicated in the inner portion of the virago sleeves (see Italy, sixteenth century, p. 146) belonging to this costume.

A breast-knot, a bow of ribbon, was worn at the top of the stomacher.

Borders of lace and embroidery formed an edging known as purles.

The ruff was gradually displaced by a wide spreading collar of lace stretched on wires, opening in front and standing well off from the shoulders to show the neck. Shoulder capes had high standing collars.

Gloves had embroidered backs and were heavily perfumed.

The Palisade.—A frame of wire or wicker, necessitated by the high ruff, was used. Over this was laid the hair, frizzed, curled and rolled away from the forehead, the highest point of the erection being known as the top-knot. Dyeing, in imitation of Queen Elizabeth's fiery locks, was fashionable; so also were red wigs. Spangles, bugles and beads were used for decoration.

Headgear and Ornamentation.—Hats, corresponding in shape to those of the men, were trimmed with bunches of feathers held by jewels. The French hood of silk or velvet tightly framing the face was popular, also the caul of gold wire, cloth of gold, pearls, etc. A stuff called cyprus was used for veils.

Make-up was used by fashionables of both sexes, calling down the condemnation of clergy and the ever busy reformers. Masks were used at the theatre and on the streets.

Jewelry was worn in profusion. Several ropes of pearls, or double gold chains, were placed about the throat with the standing lace collars; such necklaces were called "esclavage." The stomacher was covered with jewels.

Handkerchiefs were also referred to as napkins and mokadors; those carried by children, muckinders.

The Venetian flag fan became a fad; other fans of feathers, straw or silk were circular in form with precious stones set in the handles attached to gold and silver chains.

Footgear.—Shoes of velvet or leather had pointed toes, their heels growing high by the end of the reign. Slashing, embroidery in gold or silver, and jeweled decoration were much used on them.

Moiles.—The cork-soled shoes from two to ten inches in height were borrowed from Venice, where they were known as the chopines. Shakespeare mentions the chopine in "Hamlet," although this is an anachronism.

Pantoffles (also pantobles) were slippers worn over velvet shoes in the street.

Night caps of gold and silver lace decorated with spangles were in Queen Elizabeth's wardrobe. Anne Boleyn's "night dress" of black satin is said to have been a dressing gown.

Materials.—Calico was a cotton fabric imported in 1549 from Calcutta; cambric, from Cambrai, France, used for handkerchiefs, ruffs, collars and shirts; calimanco, glazed linen; tuftafata, a taffety with nap like velvet; chintz, printed India cotton; corduasoy, thick silk; muslin, thin Eastern stuff; changeable taffeta; jersey; holland (holland cloth), a linen used for shirts by the rich; mokkadoes, woolen cloth; beads, in great demand for ornamentation; bombasin, silk and wool mixed at first, afterward all silk and called bombazine, manufactured at Norwich in 1575; boratto, another name for bombasin; bone lace, originally made in Flanders with bobbins of sheep's trotters, or fishbones as pins (disputed); parchment lace, resembling guipure; sussapine, a silk; broadcloth; carrels, silk and worsted mixed; cashmere, delicate stuff from Cashmere; cheverill, kid leather.

Stockings were manufactured of worsted in 1564; by 1596 they were of silk, swanskin (thin, fleecy stuff), crewell, "thred," "jarnsey," etc.

Patterns were punched or pounced (pricked) on leather.

Coventry blue, also a shade called bice, was very popular.

For the lower classes, buffin, a coarse cloth; burels, brown cloth; tawdry, cheap lace; kersey, narrow, woolen cloth; kerseymere; galloon, worsted lace in colors, originally used by peasants (later of gold and silver and worn as decoration by the rich) ; lockram, a coarse linen; caddis, a trimming of worsted and crewell used by servants; caddis garters worn by country folk; vandelas, varieties of canvas; budge, fur still used on city livery.

"Guarded" meant edged with, or having the seams covered by guards of gold and silver lace.

The middle class was permitted to wear velvet only in sleeves.

Mutch was an old woman's cap; cassock, a long-sleeved garment buttoned up the front, part of a rustic's dress resembling a smock (also in the seventeenth century) ; shoes, "well-nailed" in 1658; dudde, a coarse woolen wrapper (hence "duds").

Armor was painted russet in the sixteenth and seventeenth centuries to save cleaning and to protect it from rust.

Some people of dramatic interest during the century were: Martin Luther, Catherine of Aragon, Anne Boleyn, Thomas Cranmer, Sir John Moore, Jane Seymour, Anne of Cleves, Catherine Howard, Catherine Parr, Thomas Cromwell, Cardinal Wolsey, Pope Leo X, Shakespeare, Spenser, Bacon, Francis Drake, Lady Jane Grey, Mary, Queen of Scots, Sir Walter Raleigh, Lord Darnley, Robert Dudley, Earl of Leicester, Sir Martin Frobisher, David Rizzio, Bothwell, and the Earl of Essex.

The Theatre.—Prior to the reign of Elizabeth, theatrical performances were given by royal command in castles, on flimsy platforms erected at fairs, or in the courtyards of inns. Productions of this kind were still being made at the Boar's Head, Ludgate Hill, The Bull, etc., when the first building for housing the drama was erected and called "The Theatre," in 1570.

Some attempt at correctness in costuming was made, for an old inventory of a theatre of Shakespeare's time mentions among other things "a freyer's gown of grey," cap and bells for fools, and "clown's sewtes."

The actors painted their faces in imitation of the fashion of the day.

CHAPTER XX

VENETIAN COSTUME

ARIOUS authorities (Charles Knight among them) set 1581 as the date for the action of "The Merchant of Venice." Cortez, a Spaniard, conquered Mexico in 1520 and Shylock speaks of his argosy sailing from this country, with which Antonio traded— "He hath a third at Mexico." The play was written in 1598.

Vecellio, a brother of Titian, wrote a book in 1589 dealing with Venetian costume; this is recommended for all plays about the Venice of Shakespeare. Abbey, the American artist, illustrated "The Merchant of Venice." His costumes are free from the stiff lines of the times, and, by means of artistic license discreetly applied, make for more attractive stage pictures.

Venice was a law unto itself in the matter of fashion, the ruff, save a very small one, being practically eliminated and the breeches without bombast. Vecellio says that through the slashes in the latter, which were cut in the form of stars and crosses, could be seen the lining of colored taffeta. Abbey dresses his Bassanio merely in a satin doublet like the old cote-hardie and full length silken tights with leather soles.

Very young lovers wore velvet caps, silk cloaks, stockings and Spanish morocco shoes, and carried a flower in one hand with gloves and a handkerchief in the other. At the age of twenty they put on a long gown with wide sleeves called a comito.

PLATE XXVIII. COSTUMES FOR "THE MERCHANT OF VENICE"

A. Costume worn by Henry Irving as Shylock (from an old photo-graph).

B. The gaberdine of Edwin Forrest (from an old photograph).

C. Shoe worn by Forrest as Othello (from old photograph).

D and E. Sleeves worn by Ethel Barrymore as Portia (drawings after photographs by White).

F. Sleeve worn by Portia in David Warfield's production of "The Merchant of Venice" (from a photograph by Alfred Cheney Johnston).

The Doge on days sacred to the Holy Virgin was dressed all in white with an ermine cape reaching to the waist. His cap, shaped like the Phrygian, always corresponded in color to that of his robe, which varied, according to the occasion, from cloth of gold or silver to crimson velvet.

Chiefs of the Council of Ten and Magistrates of Venice wore gowns of red cloth, camlet or damask, with long sleeves turned back over the wrist like those of the houppelande, and a long flap of the same material laid over the left shoulder. Stockings and slippers corresponded in color.

The Ten were robed entirely in black, save for a tiny falling band of white, one inch in width, about the neck. Very long and wide-sleeved gowns were worn over the doublet and hose. A flap of taffeta crossed the left shoulder; the cap was of felt and brimless.

A doctor of laws, according to Vecellio, always dressed in black damask cloth, velvet or silk with a sash of silk, the end hanging down to the middle of the leg. Despite this, Portia usually wears a red gown in the trial scene.

Citizens, doctors, merchants and lawyers ordinarily wore beltless robes of black cloth with ribbons of black moire over the shoulder. The garment was fastened at the neck by a pin of silver or iron. Doublet and breeches were of moire or satin.

The law of Venice required a Jew to wear a yellow bonnet of a tawny shade. There is a story that the color originally was scarlet, but changed after a Jew had been mistaken for a cardinal. However, in England from the days of Richard I, the customary headdress had been a yellow cap. The form of the Venetian cap was identical with that of the black one worn by the Christian merchants. Shakespeare speaks of Shylock's Jewish gaberdine, a garment variously described. For stage use it is often cassocklike in form with long hanging sleeves permitting the doublet-covered arm to pass through a slit at the elbow. The decoration consists of horizontal bars placed the length of the garment, each terminating in a button. With it is worn a sash from which a leather money pouch depends.

Shylock's beard is usually red, for the tale has it that Burbage, often at Kenilworth Castle where his father was stationed, saw and copied the tawny beard of Dr. Lopez, Elizabeth's Jewish physician, when creating Shylock.

An Italian doublet was always cut running to a low point in front. Striped material placed to run in circles, a touch typically Venetian, formed the tight forearm sleeves. For his gallants, Abbey uses the one-armed drape, which always allows of many graceful curves.

The hair of young men was cut round with curled ends, the bang being frizzed. It has been described in a play of the period as looking like "a half moon in a mist."

For women, Abbey makes use of the simarre. The varied sleeves admit of puffing and slashing at shoulder and elbow. When wing sleeves are used the inner tight-fitting one is often striped horizontally; these accompanying round, full skirts opening in front to show a petticoat worn with or without the farthingale.

Cauls of gold and pearls decorated the hair. Long veils of transparent silk reaching to the ground were of white for young girls, yellow for Jewish women, and of black for wives and widows. This last color was seized upon by courtesans in imitation of those respectable women. However, it is said that the chopines, shoes with cork soles twelve inches high or more and fashionable in Constantinople, were first worn in Venice by these ladies. The craze for them died out in Venice in 1670, spreading later all over Europe, even to England.

Vecellio says that besides their yellow veils the Jewesses were heavily painted; otherwise their costume corresponded to that of the Christian women.

The flag-shaped fan was Venetian. In Venice as well as in other Italian cities, very high flaring collars of lace were worn on dresses, and of a self-material on cloaks. These stood up across the shoulders with the center portion bent forward and caught down on the head in a fashion resembling the Mary Stuart cap. The portrait of Marie de' Medici by Rubens in the Prado, Madrid, offers a striking example of this style; the high black collar on the cloak is arched over a widespread wired one of white.

The Council of Ten wore masks. A fad for these disguises spread among the citizens. Worn with dominoes which were of all materials and colors, wide-sleeved and with hooded shoulder cape, the wearer could mingle in the wildest parties without fear of recognition.

Venetian lace enriched with gold and silver has always been of great beauty.

Both "Othello" and "Twelfth Night" are located in Venice at this period. "The Taming of the Shrew" calls for Italian costuming of Shakespeare's time. Katherine usually wears a farthingale and virago sleeves. Ada Rehan used a caul on her bobbed wig.

CHAPTER XXI

THE SEVENTEENTH CENTURY

THE RUSSIANS

OR the czar the costume consisted of a tunic to the ankles with fitted shoulders; a collar and full sleeves of elaborate brocade; a heavily jeweled cross of gold on a chain about the neck; a cap edged with fur with a conical top surmounted by a cross.

The Russian boot of variously colored leathers, fitting the foot snugly, wrinkling in folds about the ankles, and reaching either halfway up the calf or finished with wide tops extending over the knee and held to the leg by a leather strap buckled below it, was worn by all classes. It was usually without fastening, being pulled on like a riding boot.

MEN

A belted tunic or blouse reached to well below the knee with either elbow or long sleeves, showing a shirt of contrasting color in the wide V-neck opening. Over the tunic, sometimes a long well fitting coat had its two front flaps folded back to the belt line in a fashion identical with that of the Turks. The cap was fur-bordered with a conical crown of velvet or cloth.

For both men and women, full length cloaks were caught together at the neck, then hung loose showing the blouse or gown beneath. Some were cut with arm-

179

holes and hanging over them was a cape running in a deep curve down the back. All edges were bordered with fur. Showy decorations common to all garments were worn by the rich.

WOMEN

The women wore full stiffened skirts and a sleeveless jacket, whose base hung loose from the figure about the hips. Huge puffed sleeves of another material were gathered to the wrists.

A full-sleeved blouse belted or hanging loose, was about knee length; below it was a full skirt. Many colors were combined in one costume in the way of borders, stripes, bands about the shoulders and above the elbow, fancy aprons and headdresses. One of the latter, an upstanding crownlike affair of metal, often finished with a huge bow at the back of the neck, is not only very popular, but most attractive for stage purposes, admitting of much color ornamentation. Such a one has been used by Nina Tarasova, the singer.

Some headdresses resembled turbans, others domes, the latter fitting the crown of the head and surmounted by a peak or a round knob. Veils and wimples were suspended from, and thrown about them. Fur was lavishly used.

The most common form of Russian blouse is a full-sleeved tunic belted at the waist and reaching the thighs; its fullness is gathered into a narrow neckband of a contrasting material, which is also used to bind the edges of an opening about four or five inches long left on the right side of the blouse to admit of the head being easily passed through. Full trousers are tucked into high boots below the knee.

PLATE XXIX. DETAILS OF THE STUART PERIOD

A. Woman wearing a chin clout, England, James I.

B. Hair and sleeve, England, Charles I (from a portrait by Van Dyck).

C. Fanciful sleeve of Nell Gwynne (from the portrait by Sir Peter Lely).

D. The Van Dyck collar.

THE TARTARS

Much of the oriental was retained in the dress of the Tartars, the women showing below long skirts full trousers gathered about the ankles and rosetted slippers with turned-up toes; veils over tight-fitting turbans like headdresses of metal bands with silk or cloth tops; long, black hair hanging in several flat braids to the waist.

A tight-necked blouse of striped material was tucked into long, very full trousers at the waistline, where a wide striped sash was knotted. Low flat slippers were pointed and slightly turned up at the toes. The mandarin sleeves hanging in wide ends at the elbow were suspended from long, loose coats with narrow neckbands.

THE TURKS

MEN

Large turbans were elaborately rolled about a fez which rose to a high point at the crown. A long-sleeved, well fitting tunic with full skirts opened from the waist down, its two corners folded back exposing either another tunic reaching to the boot, or baggy trousers gathered into the boot-top.

WOMEN

A tight-fitting dress opened down the entire front, with sleeves smooth over the upper arm and becoming wide below the elbow; a tight inner sleeve showed on the forearm. The loose front section of the gown rounded off to display a full underskirt of another material reaching nearly to the ankle; below, baggy trousers. Elaborate borders and decorations of embroidery and jewels were lavishly used. Bands of trimming were placed in horizontal rows across the front of the dress from the very low neck line to that of the waist. Sashes and girdles slipped down over the hips and were ornamented with fringe and tassels.

Slippers were pointed.

Fringe was arranged in semicircles at each side of the headdress, which was rather round and stiff; a cockade, strings of pearls and feathers were fastened to one side with a large jewel.

Necklaces, earrings, bracelets, and a fan like the flag-shaped one of the Venetians were popular.

Veils were worn by all women.

THE JEWS

MEN

A mantle was edged with fringe with holes for the arms, its square corners decorated with tassels. A cap, closely fitting the head, had a tasseled point that fell over like that of an old-fashioned nightcap. The fringed tunic, if slit open on its sides, was also tasseled about the corners. A girdle with fringed ends knotted in front passed twice around the body.

WOMEN

A long gown, slit open up the right side to the waist, allowed an inner tunic to show. This gown was drawn up through two girdles which encircled the hips and waist respectively. A turban was wrapped about the flowing hair. Striped scarfs with fringed ends were much used, and sandals covered the feet. A chain of gold

discs worn across the forehead was allowed to hang each
side of the face.   Disc necklaces, bracelets, and veils over
the hair were other popular decorations.

THE SYRIANS

Many colors appeared in the outer garments and a multi-
plicity of stripes covered a long tunic made with a small
neckband and fastened to the waistline.   Sleeves with
loose ends fell over the wrists.   Weapons were stuck
through a belt.   Over all was a coat, wide open in front,
with elbow sleeves.   Baggy trousers were tucked into boots
reaching halfway up the calf ; the head was bound like that
of an Arab with long hair hanging to the shoulders.   A
mustache was worn.

THE ARABS OF BAGDAD

A tunic of striped material reached to the ankles, a
burnous to the middle of the calf, and the shoes were
turned up in points at the toes.   The head was bound with
"agals" of hair holding down the white haik which hung
in folds about the face and over the shoulders.   A belt held
many weapons.

THE FRENCH (FIRST HALF OF THE SEVENTEENTH CENTURY)

MEN

Baggy, slashed trunks were called "Gally-Gascoignes"
after the Gascons from Navarre.   Long hose, doublets,
and shoulder capes were worn.   Tight sleeves had epaulets ; with these a ruff.   The full outer sleeves, slashed
from shoulder to wrist, exposed inner ones, accompanied
by lace cuffs and collars.   Large plumed hats, also velvet
ones with curled-up brims and high shirred-in crowns

with a jeweled clasp holding a feather at the front or side were worn. The hat of the musketeers was always broad brimmed with long feathers over the side.

The time for "Cyrano de Bergerac" is about 1640. High leather boots fitted the leg to above the knee or were made with wide tops falling back.

"Lovelocks," sections of hair over the ear allowed to grow waist length and decorated with a bow, were affected at the beginning of the century by French courtiers.

WOMEN

A fitted bodice to which was attached a long train was worn over an undergown of a contrasting color and material distended by the farthingale. Sleeves were of the virago type. Across the shoulders a high lace collar was spread out on a wire frame. (See the portraits of Marie de' Medici painted by Rubens in 1623.)

THE SECOND HALF OF THE CENTURY

MEN

Short, square-cut jackets were worn over baggy shirts. Below appeared the Rhinegrave breeches, wide and loose with long, square-cut panels hanging over them like a shirt. These were introduced from Germany and alluded to by Molière in "Le Bourgeois Gentilhomme." (See also Petticoat Breeches, the English, seventeenth century, p. 194.) Bunches of ribbon were attached to shoulders, elbows, waist, hips, knees, even the low, square-toed, red-heeled shoes receiving clusters on their sides near the toes. High, floppy boots had their wide tops full of lace frills, and, incongruously, spurs at the ankles.

Either a tall crowned hat with a curling brim decorated

with feathers drooping over the right shoulder was worn or a broad-brimmed one with a long plume like that of the musketeer.

Broad, white collars appeared on a high band, but no ruffs. Lace or linen cravats were tied across with stiff strings.

Gauntlet gloves were worn.

Shoulder Knots.—Anne of Austria presented one to Buckingham, with a diamond attached to every point in the great bunch of ribbon.

Louis XIV is said to have had beautiful hair as a boy, which was allowed to cascade down his back. Wigs in imitation were introduced and worn by courtiers. They became an established fashion in France in 1660, although not adopted by the King until several years later. Mme. de Maintenon's sway over Louis made itself felt even in the matter of clothes, those of the men becoming very quiet, almost plain, by the end of the century.

WOMEN

The gowns, with skirts that trailed on the ground, which necessitated the lifting of them in front, were cut extremely low, almost to the waistline in the back, and worn off the rouged shoulders. A trimming common to France and Spain was an edging fashioned of another material and color put on full and caught together at regular intervals. Jewels were used for the latter and also served to catch up the full, slashed sleeve about the elbow.

Flowers were worn in the hair. Ladies stuck them in glass bottles filled with water and hidden in their curls.

The Manteau.—This was a bodice with a train attached,

the latter looped over a bustle of gummed cloth which crackled at every movement, and was called a "criarde" in consequence. The sleeves, either tight fitting to the elbow, or fan-shaped, were edged with lace ruffles called "engageants." The flouncings and ruchings on the skirt were termed "falbalas," while stripes of various colors sewn on as borders became "pretantailles." This garment appeared toward the end of the century, after men had adopted the coat, and in time became known as the Watteau. (See sack-back, the English, eighteenth century, p. 215.)

The engageant sleeve on the manteau was supreme until about 1780.

The Fontange.—The women's hair, which had been arranged in a curled, pearl-strung coiffure with ringlets bobbing over the bare shoulders, underwent a decided change. In 1680, Mlle. de la Fontange, a lady in waiting at the court of Louis XIV, was thrown from her horse while hunting and her hair fell down. She tied it up with her garter. This started the fashion of the fontange, an erection composed of lace, ribbons, ruffles and flutings raised one above another on a wire frame to the height of some eighteen inches; it was placed on the head tilted slightly forward over the forehead curls. The hair was coiled behind it, with one or two long curls hanging over the shoulder. The fontange is used in all of Molière's plays.

Taking snuff from personal boxes was a French fashion.

Earrings were worn by men.

Muffs, originating in France in the late sixteenth century, continued in use for a long while; at first they were made of various expensive materials and trimmed with lace and ribbons.

The Theatre.—The French stage received the greatest literary contributions in its history during the seventeenth century. Due to the patronage of Cardinal Richelieu, who himself had aspirations as a playwright and maintained two theatres in the Palais Royal, actors flourished. "Le Cid," by Corneille, produced in 1636, was quickly followed by the works of Racine and later by those of Molière, all so great that to this day they are retained in the repertoire of the Comédie Française.

The Cid lived in Spain in the eleventh century, but it is interesting to note that French tragediennes when essaying the rôle of Chimène, must have worn the enormous farthingales so fashionable in France and in Spain about the date of the play's first performance. These have been immortalized by Velasquez in his portraits of the Infanta and her family. It is hard to believe that the Phèdres and the Iphigénies preferred them to the clinging, graceful lines of the Grecian gown, but Planché tells us that all French tragediennes wore full skirts and hoops from the days of Corneille well into the eighteenth century.

Reigning monarchs during the century were Henry IV, Louis XIII (1610-1643), and Louis XIV (1643-1715) in France; and Philip IV in Spain.

People of the Continent of dramatic interest were: Cardinal Richelieu, Cardinal Mazarin, La Fontaine, Racine, Corneille, Molière; Mignard, Rembrandt, Velasquez, Zurbaran, Murillo, Guido Reni, Giordano, Tiepolo, Guercino, Teniers, Franz Hals, Jordaens; Calderon, Covarrubias, the Duke of Olivares, Don Juan of Austria; Marie de' Medici, Condé, Turenne, Pascal, Fénelon,

PLATE XXX. SEVENTEENTH-CENTURY SILHOUETTES

A. The cavalier (from the portrait of Charles I by Van Dyck).

B. The farthingale, France, time of Cardinal Richelieu (drawing from a photograph of Alma Rubens in "Under the Red Robe").

C. The age of ribbons, petticoat breeches, England, Charles II.

Mme. de Sevigné, Mlle. de la Vallière, Mme. de Montespan and Mme. de Maintenon.

THE ENGLISH: JAMES I, 1602-1625

MEN

A close-fitting doublet with tight sleeves was worn with trunks wide and full; some enormous ones of Dutch origin were referred to as "slops" by Shakespeare. Bombasting was carried to extremes, but slashing was going out of style. Large plain collars or falling bands were popular; ruffs were still seen, but smaller. Roses perched on the toes of shoes, and hats with broader brims were used.

Jerkins of buff leather, one-eighth of an inch thick, were worn by soldiers in 1607 and placed under the armor after 1632. They used a buff leather coat after 1585.

Masks called "vizards" were fashionable.

A periwig known as the "Gregorian" was classed as "grave" in 1615.

WOMEN

The farthingale was still used and a bodice very stiff and cut low was accompanied by a ruff about the throat. Beaver hats were trimmed with plumes or roses.

The hair was worn off the forehead, and, in 1612, powdered with orris. Artificially produced white hair was the mode in 1621.

Painting the face was still in vogue. In 1607, women had "ceruss" cheeks (probably no worse than orange!). A pot of "ceruss" is mentioned in a play of 1615, as a cosmetic used by men for enhancing the natural bloom of the cheeks.

Muffs were called "snuftkins" or "snoskyns" early in the reign.

CHARLES I, 1625-1649; THE STUART PERIOD

This was one of the most beautiful in the history of clothes. Van Dyck's portrait of Charles depicts for us the cavalier in all his grace of costume. His portrait of himself shows the tiny and carefully brushed Carolean mustache, and hair hanging loosely to the shoulders. The pointed chin beard which reappears on so many canvasses by this artist is known to this day as the Van Dyck. The points on wide lace collars and cuffs received the same appellation.

MEN

The doublet no longer stiff and with a much higher waistline was pointed in front and finished with a narrow sash. Large sleeves were slashed from shoulder to wrist. Only two or three long slashes were placed on the doublet each side of its center opening just below the collar. This last, also that on the shirt, was often left negligently unfastened. (See Van Dyck's portrait of himself.)

Breeches were loose to the knees, where they were tied with bunches of ribbon whose tagged or pointed ends became known as "fancies." Silk stockings were no longer a novelty.

Footgear.—Shoes with broad toes were bedecked with jeweled roses or clusters of ribbon. High-heeled boots of soft leather fitted the leg. Others had very wide tops which fell back in folds, the opening thus made being filled with a frilling of lace; spurs on the ankles, and over the instep a broad band of leather. On jack boots, worn as part of the armor now mostly of leather, was a wide strip above the knee.

Hats.—Large and dashing hats had broad brims over which hung long ostrich plumes.

Voluminous cloaks of light-colored satin were draped over one shoulder. Lace collars and cuffs were cut in Van Dyck points. Ribbons appeared as decoration wherever possible. Bristol paste diamonds were very much the mode, and the king wore a large pearl in one ear. Gentlemen of the court affected earrings.

The Hair.—Long curls known as French lovelocks hung each side of the face.

Order of the Garter.—The color became a "celestial blue" probably due to the popularity of this shade; a surcoat and hood of crimson velvet was topped by a black hat of the same material draped with ostrich plumes; the badge, a Cross of Saint George surrounded by a garter, was worn by knights on everyday dresses; in 1629, by adding rays, at first wavy and subsequently straight, a form resulted which became the permanent Star of the Garter.

WOMEN

All stiffness had gone from the dress. The waist was laced with ribbon across its front opening, through which an underbodice of the same color as the petticoat could be seen. The waistline was defined by a narrow ribbon tied in a cluster of loops at one side. Below it a series of square tabs finished the bodice. The sleeves were large, either elbow length or long, and slashed open with cuffs cut in Van Dyck points. A wide lace collar encircled the shoulders of the low-cut waist. The skirt was round and full. This was the principal gown of the reign. Ribbon ends finished with metal tags known as "points," also "fancies," were the most popular form of ornamentation.

Hats were wide brimmed and trimmed with feathers. Patches on the face were the fashion. Long gloves were worn and large muffs carried. Ribbon roses on the toes of slippers were decorated with jewels.

The Hair.—It was worn parted in the middle and caught up in a knot at the back. Across the forehead was a row of small curls resembling inverted question marks; large curls descended each side of the face to the shoulders.

Chin cloths or mufflers known as "clouts" were worn by poorer women. Satin was the most popular material and ribbon rosettes a much used form of ornamentation. Red heels were seen.

The Puritans.—The reform that cost Charles his head descended on the costume also and we find the Puritans garbed in a wardrobe regulated by law.

CROMWELL, 1649-1660

The costume for both men and women was stripped of nearly all trimming and sober colors such as black, dark brown and gray were used. Plain wide linen collars and broad-brimmed hats with high crowns were worn.

The hair of both sexes now became suddenly straight and plainly arranged under linen caps; dark hoods were often attached to full-length capes.

The men had exceedingly wide tops on their boots, however, and women were permitted shoe rosettes. The strangest reform in dress was the removal of all square tabs from a woman's bodice save the one exactly in the center of the back, which hung tail-like, suggesting a possible missing link.

CHARLES II, 1660-1685

MEN

Petticoat Breeches.—During the first part of his reign, Charles and his court followed the fashion of the Rhinegraves then the vogue in France; these became known in England as "petticoat breeches." Short jackets allowed a full white blouse to hang over the beribboned waistline; the breeches were loose and bagged about the knees; skirt pieces, resembling a slit tunic, hung over them.

The Age of Ribbons.—A craze for this form of decoration developed. Bunches were used to ornament the tunic, sleeves, waistline and the leg below each knee. Clusters were tied to canes, and formed wide, stiff bows across the instep of the square-toed, high-heeled shoes with their upstanding tongues.

Hats were very large with stiff brims and decorated with feathers in profusion.

The Periwig.—The huge French peruke was not copied by Charles until his dark hair became streaked with gray; the year 1663 marked his appearance in a very large brown one of many curls, which rose in points each side of the center parting and hung thence upon the breast in two long ringlets. Such wigs were worn over armor in portraits by Lely and Kneller.

Wigs.—A powdering of meal was placed on the enormous periwigs, which began to assume various shapes.

The vallancy wig, white and full, was mentioned in 1672
and 1674 by Dryden, who also alludes to another with a
tail one yard long as "the snake." The campaign, for
traveling use, was almost as large as the periwig and differed chiefly in being flatter on top with the two long front
curls twisted into tight tails, one hanging each side of the
face and called pole locks. The rest of the hair was arranged in one tail down the back, the first hint of the bob
wig of the future. A quantity of powder was now used on
wigs. At home, on removal of these huge head coverings,
white caps were worn against draughts, as most men had
shaven heads.

Combing the periwig in public had been a popular diver-
sion in public ever since its first introduction, men being
supplied with combs for this purpose. The practice was
indulged in at the French court and was considered the
proper thing in England, the fashion lasting until Queen
Anne's reign. In Killigrew's play "The Parson's Wedding" (1663), occurs a stage direction for a group of
fashionable gentlemen which reads, "they comb their
heads and talk."

The small mustache was still in use, also the imperial
of the Frenchman.

The Coat.—The long vest of black cloth or velvet
reaching to the knees, worn by Charles in 1666 and said
to have been copied from a garment of the Russian am-
bassador, proved the first gun of the frock coat to be.
So revolutionary a style caused a sensation, but by 1670
a coat and vest had developed, and in 1679 Charles II,
according to an inventory of the time, owned a suit com-
prising "coat, waistcoat and breeches." Thus was established a new era in the body covering of man.

Cravats.—Neck cloths had ends of rich lace falling in broad folds on the chest.   They were also known as "bands," and the long ends of lace and ribbon, when used to secure them, "band strings"; the latter, when made of stout silk tasseled cords and allowed to hang limp, were named "snake-bone band strings."   The extremely large cloths were called by Dryden "bib cravats."   A fold of cambric about the throat, with long ends of point lace, was worn by George Villiers, Duke of Buckingham.

WOMEN

The Age of Satin.—Petticoats, trains and cloaks were made of this material; great elbow sleeves were slit open to show the arm beneath.   The round, very low-cut waist was worn off the shoulders.   High, red-heeled shoes had square toes and a little tongue of leather standing up above the instep in an impertinent manner.   Shorter skirts were introduced by Nell Gwynne, permitting the shoe to show.

Shoulder knots, bunches of ribbon or lace, were worn on the shoulders.   Plumed hats and patches were fashionable. Gloves were perfumed with scents from Paris.

Masks and hoods were worn always in the street and to the theatre, to which as a rule only "ladies of the evening" dared go.   See quips in plays of the day.   Pope speaks of the "masked ladies."

The Hair.—Ringlets were held out over the ear by a wire cage.   Little curls, known as "heart-breakers" and "favorites," fell across the forehead; an arrangement resembling that on the center of a bull's brow was called a "taure."   Strings of pearls were looped through the hair, ribbons clustering in the side ringlets.   Long curls were brought forward over the shoulder.

PLATE XXXI. HEADDRESSES AND SHOES, STUART AND JACOBEAN
PERIODS

A. Hat, periwig and cravat, England, Charles II.
B and D. Hat and sleeve, James II.
C and E. Commode and shoe, William and Mary.
F. Shoe with a rose of lace, Charles I.
G and H. High boots, Charles I.

See the portraits of Lady Castlemaine, the Countess of Shrewsbury, and Mrs. Hyde by Lely.

JAMES II, 1685-1689

MEN

The coat, with wide cuffs, opened in front, disclosing a long waistcoat with pockets. Braid was much used as decoration and claret color began to be popular. Breeches were snug fitting and buttoned at the side of the leg. Swords were carried in a baldrick. Shoes had buckles.

WOMEN

A black silk apron with a bib was the latest cry, worn over a full skirt, the tight bodice showing a wide collar about the shoulders. The sleeves were cuffed. Black hooded shoulder capes were used as wraps.

Plumpers, round light balls intended to fill out sunken cheeks, were a fad at the end of the reign.

WILLIAM AND MARY 1689-1702

MEN

The coat was several inches longer than the brocaded waistcoat, with sleeves half a yard wide at the elbow; the cuffs, broader still, were turned back, and, like the flaps on the pockets which were set vertically and horizontally, fastened with buttons. Two more buttons placed halfway of the coat's length caught it together. Braiding and gold fringe were much used as decoration and claret color was the rage.

The sword was fastened through the side flaps of the coat to a belt worn about the waistcoat.

PLATE XXXII. FRENCH AND RUSSIAN COSTUMES,
SEVENTEENTH CENTURY

A and E. A French cavalier and a Russian nobleman.
B and C. A French couple, showing the first coat, 1663.
D. The age of ribbons and petticoat breeches.
F and G. A French couple at the end of the century.

The Steinkirk.—This cravat had its very long ends twisted in spiral effect and drawn through a ring; occasionally they were caught through a buttonhole of the coat. Snuff boxes were considered a necessity. Canes swung from ribbon loops about the wrist, and small muffs were carried on ribbons. The stocking was pulled up over the knee and rolled, a garter holding it below. Square-toed shoes had stiffened strings and upstanding tongues, as in the previous reign.

The Cocked Hat.—This was achieved by turning up the brim of the wide hat so long popular; on one side only at first, then on two and finally on all three. Gold lace was festooned about the edges.

WOMEN

The Commode.—The appearance of the fontange (see the French, seventeenth century, p. 187), or commode as it became known in England, was a striking note in women's ever-changing attire. Tiers of lace, rising to the height of twelve inches, were fastened one above the other on a wire frame covered with a thin silk such as "tiffany," and set well forward on the head. The hair was parted in the middle, forming small curls over the temples called "confidents," and then drawn into a knot on the crown of the head behind the commode, with long curls falling over one shoulder. High lace caps were also worn with falls of lace each side of the face.

The elbow sleeve with a ruffle of lace became an established fashion. A black silk apron was worn on all gowns.

An overgown well laced in the bodice was looped over the hips on small hoops, its back ballooning down over the trained underskirt. The trimming of ribbons and ruches

PLATE XXXIII. Costumes of the Middle Class,
Seventeenth Century

A and B. A Danish couple early in the century.
C and D. Englishwomen, early and late in the century.
E and F. A German couple, 1610.
G and H. Englishman and Frenchman, 1690.

on the skirt was called "fal-lals," probably a contraction of the French falbalas. The black silk shoulder cape, small muffs, patches and make-up were all in fashion. Flat wooden soles called "clogs" were fastened to the soles and heels of the long, square-toed shoes in the street. Various new materials had appeared during the century. A la mode was a thick silklike lutestring, loosely woven; tiffany, a thin transparent silk; tabbinet, poplin; persian, thin lining silk; mochado, mock velvet; shag, shaggy cloth with a nap on one side like that of velvet, generally worsted but sometimes of silk, and used for lining; cloths such as cartmells, caltons, durance (coarse and durable); duffel, rough woolen cloth sent to America; dimity, stout linen cloth first made at Damietta; linen cloth made from flax manufactured in England; sergedusoy, coarse silken stuff for coats of common people; mary-muffe, coarse common cloth used for chin clouts by peasant women from 1604-1640.

The Theatre.—Masques by Ben Jonson, Beaumont and Fletcher, Massinger and others, were very popular early in the seventeenth century.

Inigo Jones left costume designs for the Morris dancers and harlequinades, also one for Romeo as a pilgrim in the conventional long cloak with wide sleeves, shoulder cape and broad-brimmed hat. For the Morris dancers, the costume is that of Elizabeth, gaily colored, embroidered, feathered and hung with bells.

When the Globe Theatre was burnt in 1613, a poem of the day alluded to the lost "perriwigs" and jerkins. Another, when the cockpit in Drury Lane was pillaged, states that "King Priam's robes were soon in rags."

However, a print of the time of Charles II represents

Dame Quickly and Falstaff making merry in the dress of 1660, proving that actors were given to serious lapses in the matter of correct costuming.

At the end of the seventeenth century, during the reign of William and Mary, the custom of peopling plays with fantastic and mythological characters went into disuse.

People of dramatic interest were Guy Fawkes; George Villiers, Duke of Buckingham (killed by Felton); George Villiers, Duke of Buckingham, son of the former and favorite of Charles II; George Fox, founder of the Quakers; Betterton, the actor; Milton, Davenant, Cowley, Ben Jonson, Inigo Jones; Jean Bart; Van Dyck; Dryden, Beaumont, Defoe, Bunyan, Samuel Pepys, Massinger; Pocahontas, Lady Castlemaine, Nell Gwynne and the Countess of Shrewsbury.

The date for the Cavaliers and Roundheads is 1642. The opera of "Gioconda" is laid in Venice during the century, while "Traviata" takes place at Paris about 1700. (The play "Camille," by Alexandre Dumas *fils,* and founded upon the same story, is dated in the middle of the nineteenth century and modern clothes are requested by the author.) "Ruy Blas" is laid in Spain, 1692.

CHAPTER XXII

THE EIGHTEENTH CENTURY

THE FRENCH

MEN

THE coat changes were identical with those described for the English (see the English, eighteenth century). Just before the French Revolution its tails were ankle length. About 1794 the so-called *"Incroyables"* affected enormous stocks well up over the chin, resembling the barbes worn by women in the sixteenth century; cocked hats like Napoleon's accompanied them.

The Solitaire.—A ribbon of black silk tied loosely around the neck of gentlemen made its début at the court of Louis XV. It was sometimes fastened to the bag of the wig.

Muffs, decorated with large bows of ribbon, were carried by men as well as women. French abbés had black ones to match their costumes. For wigs, see the English, eighteenth century, pp. 208 and 214.

WOMEN

The fontange lingered from the previous century, despite the protests of Louis XIV, until the appearance in 1714 of an Englishwoman wearing the low headdress so popular at Queen Anne's court; whereupon the towers which had reigned so long were immediately discarded by

PLATE XXXIV. THE DEVELOPMENT OF THE COAT

A and B. The coat as it appeared in 1710 and 1720.
C. During the reigns of Louis XV and George II.
D and E. Cutaway after 1765 and very long in 1785.
F. A topcoat and beaver hat in 1835.

the women of France, who proceeded to copy the English fashion—a rare occasion in history, by the way.

The Pompadour.—The hair was brushed straight up from the brow over a pad, a style much in vogue during the middle of the century and named for the favorite of Louis XV. (This fashion in an exaggerated form was revived by the Gibson girl toward the end of the nineteenth century.) To match the solitaire of the men, a black velvet ribbon was worn about the neck, a small ruching being occasionally substituted.

The Watteau gown, cut with a square neck and panniers and affected by Mme. de Pompadour, was made with an all-over design of exquisitely colored flowers giving rise to the term "pompadour silk."

The equipage or étui, a case containing a thimble, scissors, etc., was worn by ladies at the left side of the waist early in the century.

The hoop was not modish in France until 1718; whether this fashion was borrowed from England, Germany or the stage is a disputed point. Huge pocket hoops, or panniers in exaggerated form, were discarded by Marie Antoinette in 1782, in favor of a full skirt bustled at the back.

Powder was used in the hair until just prior to the Revolution.

The Theatre.—Addison held up to ridicule the costuming indulged in by the French theatre. The enormous hoops used by women at the beginning of the century are said to have been copied from those worn by French actresses, who since the days of Corneille had persisted in playing tragic rôles in full skirts. The reform, instigated by Voltaire and carried to success by Mlle. Clairon, met with strong opposition from the players. That a reform was needed goes without saying, if we may judge by a drawing made at the end of the seventeenth century portraying, in a French play of the day, a character called "America." This "Miss America" wears a low-cut bodice with engageant sleeves, ballet skirts, a long train hanging from her shoulders and high-heeled buskins laced on her bare legs; a headdress of ostrich plumes and heron feathers surmounts her hair, which hangs in ringlets on her shoulders. Evidently, in order to give an American Indian touch, she was supplied with bow and arrows. A close survey fails to reveal a tomahawk.

The characters of Pierrot, Scaramouche, Harlequin and Columbine made their appearance on the French stage early in the eighteenth century. They had long been popular in Italy, where the old man known as Pantaloon, a Venetian creation, was also a prime favorite. However, this "slippered pantaloon" was never used in France. The costumes for these famous characters of pantomime have remained practically the same to this day.

The time for "Adrienne Lecouvreur" is 1730; "Manon," the second half of the century; "Tosca," 1800 (in Italy).

People of dramatic interest in France and other continental countries were:

Voltaire, Quentin Latour (see pastels of court beauties), Nattier; Mme. Le Brun, Mme. Récamier, Fragonard, Coustou, Boucher, Greuze, David; Beaumarchais, Mozart, Mme. du Barry, Mme. de Staël, Mme. Roland, Charlotte Corday; Bach, Beethoven, Handel; Lafayette, Robespierre, Mirabeau, Danton.

France was governed by: Louis XIV, until 1715; Louis

XV, 1715-1774; Louis XVI, 1774-1793; the Republic, 1793, and Napoleon, as First Consul, 1799.

Monarchs reigning elsewhere were: Peter the Great, 1722; Catherine I of Russia, 1725; Frederick the Great of Prussia, 1712-1786.

THE ENGLISH: QUEEN ANNE, 1702-1714

MEN

The coat, pleated over the hips and standing out from the figure, was now cut a bit shorter. The black steinkirk of knotted silk, with ends either twisted or hanging loose, was the popular cravat. An amber-headed cane hung from the fifth button of the coat by a loop of blue silk ribbon. The monocle came into fashion.

Low shoes with tongues were decorated with buckles and red heels.

The Ramillies Wig.—Wigs were worn by all classes including countrymen, the formal periwig and the campaign wig holding undisputed sway among the fashionables until after the battle of Ramillies in 1706. A new style in wigs, named to celebrate the victory, was made with the white hair drawn back from the forehead, puffed out each side of the face and braided into a long pigtail, at the top of which a large velvet bow was placed, with another and much smaller at the bottom. It was at first considered informal, and an anecdote recounts that Lord Bolingbroke presented himself in one before Queen Anne, who, much affronted, remarked that he would doubtless appear next in his nightcap. (The hat worn with this wig was called the Ramillies cock.)

Much time and attention were given the care of wigs.

PLATE XXXV. A SCENE FROM "MONSIEUR BEAUCAIRE"

France during the reign of Louis XV (first half of the eighteenth century). A scene from the photoplay "Monsieur Beaucaire," in which Valentino wore unpowdered hair and Bebe Daniels the huge panniers of this period.

Roulettes (in French, bilbouquettes) were heated clay tubes like pipe stems, three or four inches long, round which the hair was wound and there held in place by twisted papers. This process was called putting the wig "in buckle." Whitening the hair, often with scented powder, had become general. A glass cone was held over the mouth and nose while the hairdresser dusted on the powder. In a scene of the photoplay, "Orphans of the Storm," Joseph Schildkraut's wig is whitened by a *perruquier*. In the country men gathered their own hair in loose bunches or "bobs" at the sides, tying it in a twisted pigtail behind. The bob wig, copying the bushy hair over the countryman's ear, was introduced.

WOMEN

Small aprons were trimmed with gold lace and spangles.

The hair was left its natural color; on it the fontange reposed, shrunk to a tiny ruffle like the one worn on the heads of housemaids of to-day.

In 1711 heavy canvas petticoats, stiffened with whalebone to a tremendous size, formed hoop skirts. The bodice was square cut and tight fitting in front, with a loose back looped over a full skirt. Tight elbow sleeves finished with lace ruffles. Red heels, tall walking sticks, and patches in profusion—the politics of the wearer being proclaimed by the location of the last named—were the mode.

Full masks suspended from the waist by a ribbon were adopted by ladies when riding. Small ones covering the nose were called "loo masks"; during this reign their use was prohibited.

PLATE XXXVI. MRS. JOHN DREW AS MRS. MALAPROP IN
"THE RIVALS"

The scene of the opera "Martha" is England during Queen Anne's reign.

GEORGE I, 1714-1727
MEN

Coats were shorter still and very full at the sides.

A wig with three queues (tails) was fashionable.

Stockings were rolled over the knees, those of blue or scarlet silk clocked in gold or silver being favored by the beaux. Shoes had large buckles. The hat was cocked, being now turned up abruptly on three sides.

Cretonne was first used in this reign.

WOMEN

Pointed shoes with high heels were worn.

Lace caps were substituted for the fontange. Panniers were larger. The equipage was worn. (See the French, eighteenth century, p. 206.)

GEORGE II, 1727-1760
MEN

The wide skirts of the coats were stiffened with buckram and wire, which held them out from the figure in a jaunty fashion. Enormous embroidered cuffs were similarly treated. Lace was used to trim the coats.

The Chapeau-Bras.—A flat-crowned hat with a cocked brim was carried under the left arm to prevent disarranging the elaborately powdered wig.

In 1730 a fringed sash called a burdash was tied about the waist.

The stockings were pulled up over the knees and rolled.

Handsome garters were placed below. Low shoes had buckles and red heels. In 1751 a pair of diamond buckles was listed as costing forty pounds.

The French fashion known as the solitaire was copied. (See the French, eighteenth century, p. 204.)

Cocked hats of every variety were worn; in 1732 the brims were seven inches wide and sometimes irregular, *i.e.*, high in the back and low in front. The angle of the cock was a matter of much concern.

Muffs of all sizes were carried by the men, including deans and doctors, not merely as an affectation but for comfort.

After 1745 the coat was worn shorter and its fullness allowed to hang in limp folds against the body with the large cuffs negligently crushed; this lack of stiffening continued until the end of the reign. From 1740-1751, a coat of light blue with silver buttonholes grew popular.

The garter was removed, and the breeches ended in a band buckled or buttoned over the stockings above the knee according to the fad of the moment.

Laces, no longer fashionable on coats, were transferred to the short, double-breasted waistcoat which now made its appearance.

Buttons.—These were in great demand owing to the quantities needed for coats, waistcoats and knee breeches. Semi-precious stones such as malachite, bloodstone, onyx, lapis lazuli, carnelian and agate, also tortoise-shell and ivory were used in their making. Wooden buttons were covered with material of which the garment was made, their tops decorated with steel beads, embroidery, crocheting and the like. Buttonholes were elaborately embroidered, tasseled and fringed.

The Banyan.—Hogarth and other artists of the time show us men wearing turbans or caps with this garment, which strongly resembled a dressing gown. It was a robe of East Indian origin fashioned of gaily figured oriental silks, crêpes, brocades, velvets or cotton fabrics. At home, and while entertaining informally, elaborate coats were removed for this showy but more comfortable article of apparel. Long, wide sleeved and without collar or revers, through its front opening could be seen lace frills, waistcoat, satin breeches with paste buckles, and red-heeled shoes. Wigs were also removed and the shaven head protected by a cap or brightly colored turban cocked to one side.

Wigs.—During this reign wigs were at the topnotch of their popularity. The enormous periwig was superseded by the tie wig, which was sponsored, like the Ramillies, by the intrepid Bolingbroke. Young men were beginning to use their own hair arranged wig fashion and powdered.

The wigs were not made or worn with any idea of deception, as is the case with modern ones, including toupees and transformations, but were simply the fashion. They were constructed often of horsehair and fine wire, quite visibly false, and frequently worn pushed awry. Those of human hair were very expensive, especially when of the full curled type. Gozzans, as they were styled when yellow with age, could be grabbed out of a hole in a cask at a wig lottery in Rosemary Lane, London.

Every variety of wig had a name, and, as each profession and trade affected a different style, the list was long.

The bag, originating with French servants, who thrust

their hair into a leather bag, was fashionable during the reign of George II.

The pigtail was worn by soldiers either hanging down or doubled back and tied. The bob was the simple wig of the poor.

Some of the names listed included the Count Saxe, rhinoceros, cauliflower (a coachman's wig), comet, levant, Grecian fly, scratch, dalmahoy, snail-back, spinach seed, Tyburn scratch, pigeon's wing, etc.

WOMEN

A tight-fitting, square-necked bodice had lace-frilled elbow sleeves. A round skirt had another looped over large panniers springing up in high wide arches on which the elbows could be rested. Long, plain aprons were worn, despite the objections of Beau Nash. The hair was pulled back to a knot on the crown; the forehead was adorned with curls. Small caps were tied or perched on the head. High-heeled shoes had pointed toes and buckles. Patches were still in vogue.

The Sack-back or Sacque (Watteau).—The beautiful gown known in France as the Watteau became popular as the sack-back in England about 1750, and did not completely go out of fashion until 1794. Made with a low, square-cut bodice tightly fitted in front, its loose back was cut full enough to allow of four box pleats being placed on the shoulder, two facing the right, and two the left. These were stitched flat to the bodice lining for a few inches, the material falling thence in balloonlike folds to about a foot from the ground; the forward breadths, which sometimes were cut to extend to the neck line, were looped over the hips or panniers (in fashion during the middle of the century). This section of the gown comprised the "sack." The elaborate petticoat worn with it was of another material and color, receiving lavish ornamentation such as lace ruffles, flounces, fancy pleatings and ruchings called furbelows. The ruffled engageant sleeve belonged to the sack, the same form of ornamentation appearing about the neck of the latter. This was one of the most beautiful costumes of all time.

The variety of sacque having an open front looped back on panniers and ending in a train was called the polonaise or slammerkin. When the fullness of the train was caught together in a twist about a foot from the ground, then allowed to hang free, the fashion was dubbed "monkey-tailed." The trollopée was a loose morning gown with an open front and gathered back, worn in 1750.

All these styles permitted a lavishly decorated petticoat of another material and contrasting color to show at the front, it being a law of this costume that the petticoat *must not match the sacque.*

The very low neck was sometimes filled in by a "modesty" of gauze. A black velvet ribbon or ruching was usually worn about the throat with the sacque.

In 1756 the hair was drawn away from the face, powdered, and puffed in a pompadour. Gradually false hair was added to it, headdresses assuming huge proportions by the end of the reign. Full white wigs were also worn.

A cap, made with circles of linen resembling wheels covering each ear, and called the "cabriolet" after a vehicle of that name imported from France in 1755, became fashionable.

GEORGE III, 1760-1820

MEN

The macaroni fashions were in vogue about 1760, small coatees cut extremely short, large lawn cravats, very tall wigs, small hats and an attempted revival of the large, loose, ribbon-trimmed breeches of Charles II, being the chief manifestations.

The solitaire was superseded by a large lawn cravat.

The coat, boasting a collar, was laced and frogged with its hitherto right-angled fronts rounded off like the modern cutaway. (These corners had been previously buttoned back for convenience by soldiers.) It was short waisted before the French Revolution, and sharply cut back like the coat of a full dress suit, with tails very long and full, and no cuffs. The collar, standing very high at the back of the neck, ended in broad revers.

The shirt was sometimes left open at the throat, with a cravat loosely tied below. Lace-edged ruffles called "chitterlings" were also used in the coat opening above the double-breasted waistcoat, which extended below the coat line. During this reign black satin knee-breeches, worn skin tight, were in fashion. A loose pair are spoken of as "bags" in the "School for Scandal." About 1790 the tight-fitting pantaloon, buttoned for several inches above the ankle, was first seen.

The greatest amount of powder was used in the hair about 1776-1777, when wigs and headdresses were at their largest. Pink powder was in vogue in 1780. About this date, wigs were smaller, with two horizontal curls over the ears, kept in shape by inserted wires; a queue or pigtail hung at the back. Powder was going out of fashion in 1785, when the hair, imitating a wig, was arranged in long pigtails. By the French Revolution, short hair and side whiskers were quite common.

The cocked hats, with a cockade in front, gradually disappeared when the natural hair came into vogue. Hats with broad brims were superseded by others with high crowns and curled edges; after the Revolution, the high beaver hat was worn.

A craze for striped clothing set in about 1793; the period was alluded to as the "zebra."

Shoes showed buckles, pointed toes and lower heels; broad tops several inches wide, turned back and faced with light brown leather, appeared on high wrinkled boots. Hessians were stiff boots running up in a point below the knee, whence the sides curved away to a lower back. The tops were finished with gold cord tied with tasseled ends in front.

Snuff boxes, also sword sticks, were carried and, in the early part of the reign, muffs.

Women

The sack-back dress was worn during the early years of the reign. In 1760 a cloak called the "cardinal," owing to its close resemblance to one worn by ecclesiastics of that title, came into style. The "Artois" was another cloak with three or four shoulder capes adopted in 1783; the lowest cape ran to a deep point in the back; lapels decorated this garment, which was noticeably "tailored," in keeping with the mannish tendency in cut so apparent on women's clothes at that time.

The High Headdress.—This resembled a tower, attaining its greatest height in 1777. Horse hair, tow, hemp

PLATE XXXVII. EIGHTEENTH-CENTURY WIGS

A. Campaign wig (from a book by Randle Holme printed in 1685).

B. The pigtail wig.

C. Wig with wired side curls.

D. The bag wig and stiffened coat skirts (from a drawing by Hogarth).

E. Wired side curls. Wig worn by Boswell in a portrait.

F. The wig of the Macaroni, 1760.

G. The court wig, usually accompanied by the solitaire (drawing from a photograph by Paramount, of Valentino as Monsieur Beaucaire).

and wool were glued together with pomatum and the hair, with false curls and puffs added, fastened up over this pad. The dressing, which concluded with powdering and scenting, required many hours, so that, except for the re-perfuming necessary, it did not have to be repeated for several weeks. At night large caps were drawn over the entire headdress, and special head rests were used as pillows to preserve the shape.

For full dress occasions, frilled white caps were placed on top of the headdress; feathers, baskets, ships, strings of pearls or ribbon loops were also used as decoration. A scarf was sometimes wound about a huge pompadour and floated from the shoulders, as in the portrait of Lady Hamilton.

In 1780 a very full skirt was held out over a bustle, accompanied by a low-necked, short-waisted bodice with wide revers. A sash was tied in a bow on the bustle. The elbow sleeves, after reigning for a century, were supplanted by long tight ones in 1785. A fichu was placed about the low neck and tied in front, terminating in frilled ends below the knees.

About 1786, by dint of lacing and much bunching of the fichu, the figure was made to resemble that of a pouter pigeon.

Headgear.—Large mob caps with enormous ribbon bows were worn and in 1787 large hats (the enormous one covered with plumes, worn by the Duchess of Devonshire in the famous Gainsborough, conveys a good impression of the fashionable size). Very tall crowns were also seen.

The Calash and the Caravan.—Two large bonnets were made with hoops of whalebone arching over the top of the head, the whole strongly resembling a covered wagon. These were invented by the Duchess of Bedford for wear with the enormous headdresses. The "caravan" was equipped with a thin veil of sarsenet, meant for screening the face in an emergency; while, by pulling a string attached to a button on the forward rib of the calash, the whole collapsible contrivance would rise up over the headdress and protect it.

Bouquets carried in flat glass bottles containing water were fastened to the waist, in 1770.

About 1790 the waistline became decidedly high and the skirt fell in limp folds. The sleeves were short and puffed at the top. After the French Revolution, dresses were cut to resemble Grecian tunics, in imitation of the fashions set by the *"Merveilleuse," i.e.,* the women of France who indulged in extreme cuts to match the men called the *"Incroyables."* Some were slit to above the knee, others looped and fastened on the left side by brooches.

High sticks were fashionable; umbrellas, used in Italy since the sixteenth century, were carried for the first time by Englishmen in 1770, the début of the parasol quickly following its adoption by the French in 1777.

Patches went into disuse after the passing of the powdered hair.

Two watches were worn, one for use, the other called a fausse montre, fashioned of brocade and heavily embroidered with gaily colored flowers in imitation of enameling. The real watch was placed on the right side, with the false one suspended by a gold cord attached to the waistline on the left.

Very large muffs were correct at the end of the century.

(See the portrait of Mme. Raymond, by Mme. Le Brun.)

Long gloves, reaching well above the elbow and worn in a series of loose folds, were in favor after the French Revolution.

Footgear.—The low shoe became slender after 1780, and developed a French heel; this disappeared with the revival of the Greek dresses at the close of the century.

The Hair.—With the revival of natural hair, that of the women was worn curled across the forehead and gathered in a knot of loose ringlets on top of the head.

Turbans were a popular form of headdress.

Materials.—New materials in use were swansdown, used for lining in jackets; sagathee, a thin stuff like serge; shalloon, a woolen lining from Chalons; poplin, a silk shot with worsted; paduasoy, an Italian silk; lutestring, corded silk; du cape, the same; catgut, stiff corded cloth used for lining, and in sleeves and skirts for stiffening.

Beaver hats, also called "castor," were worn.

Very handsome materials were commonly lined with printed cotton stuff.

The peasantry began to use straw hats; those of the women were placed over the white, ribbon-tied, mob cap.

The Theatre.—During the first half of the eighteenth century, scarcely any attention was paid to correct theatrical costuming. Mrs. Yates played Lady Macbeth in huge panniers, while Garrick, always clad in the fashion of George II, had a suit of black velvet as a special concession when appearing as Hamlet. To suggest Othello, he put some blacking on his face.

Pope speaks of "Cato's long wig, flowered gown and lacquered chair," alluding to the performance of Barton Booth in Addison's "Cato." The "flowered gown" means

PLATE XXXVIII. LATE EIGHTEENTH-CENTURY COSTUMES

A. A "shepherdess" of the Trianon, 1780.
B. A middle-class Frenchwoman in a mob cap, 1780.
C and D. The pouter pigeon in 1786 and the mannish cut in 1785.
E and F. The *"Merveilleuse"* and *"Incroyable."*

the popular banyan, and the "long wig" the enormous periwig of Queen Anne's reign.   No wonder the disgusted
author relieved himself in *The Spectator* by bitterly criti-
cizing the actors and actresses of the day for fussing
with their trains and feathers.

Garrick, due to the influence of Mlle. Clairon, whose
endeavors to change the attitude of the French regarding
correct theatrical dressing had borne fruit, produced Voltaire's "Orpheline de Chine" at Drury Lane in 1747, using
Chinese clothes.   He did not follow this up, however, for
Leigh Hunt relates an encounter between West, the portrait painter, and Garrick, wherein the former urged the
actor to pay more attention to correct clothes when dressing a part.   Garrick retorted that the spectators would
"throw a bottle at his head."   The fault seems to have
been less with the managers than with the public, who
preferred to see the players in the latest fashion of the
day (and there are, in this year 1927, hosts of women who
have no interest in a theatrical performance unless the
actresses disport themselves in the latest creations of the
Rue de la Paix.   There's a reason for the line in the pro-
gram giving credit to some one for the gowns and hats
of the leading woman).

Famous people of dramatic interest were: Churchill,
Duke of Marlborough, and Sarah, his wife; Bolingbroke;
Horace Walpole; Lady Mary Wortley Montagu; Gay;
Swift; Chatterton; Addison; Pope; Thomson; Gray;
Burns; Congreve; Goldsmith; Colly Cibber; Boswell;
Sheridan; Kneller; Hogarth; Reynolds; Romney; An-
gelica Kauffmann; Charles James Fox; Jane, Duchess of
Gordon; Sydney, Lady Morgan; Anne Seymour Damer;
Lady Caroline Lamb; Georgiana, Duchess of Devon-

shire; Jack Sheppard; Dick Turpin; Lord Nelson; Keats, Byron, Shelley and Tom Moore living at the end of the century.

The stage was represented by Barton Booth, ancestor of Edwin; Garrick, d. 1779; George Frederick Cooke, Charles Mathews; Mrs. Ann Oldfield, d. 1730; Mrs. Bracegirdle, d. 1748; Kitty Clive, d. 1785; Betterton, d. 1710; Mrs. Siddons and John Philip Kemble.

THE AMERICANS, SEVENTEENTH AND EIGHTEENTH CENTURIES

The wealthy were elegantly dressed, their clothes either imported from London or fashioned of the most expensive materials in vogue abroad. For plays dealing with this class prior to 1776, the costume of England of that period is correct.

The American Revolution curtailed supplies from the home country. Many of the younger men discarded wigs and powder somewhat earlier than was done in England; in Griffith's "America," Lionel Barrymore wore long dark curls tied with a ribbon—a wig, of course, intended to represent Major Butler's natural hair.

The clothes of the poor were warm and of serviceable materials, the chief distinction being their durability. Leather was much used for breeches, and fur for caps. Holiday clothes were expected to last the greater part of a lifetime.

CHAPTER XXIII

THE NINETEENTH CENTURY

T had become the thing for civilized nations to follow the decree of Paris in fashions. They had no radio, telegraph or telephone to transmit instantly to the furthermost corners of the globe the *dernier cri* of a Parisian modiste in the making of a sleeve, but the mail and returning travelers brought the latest wrinkle exploited by French *mondaines*. For the nineteenth century, therefore, the history of dress as adopted by the English-speaking world need alone be followed.

THE ENGLISH: THE EMPIRE PERIOD (CONTINUING THE REIGN OF GEORGE III)

Men

The coats, usually of blue cloth, were short waisted and double breasted, running to a long tail. A turned-over collar rising high above the throat ended in broad lapels. Sleeves were full at the shoulders. A waistcoat of fashionable buff color showed below the coat.

The Stock.—A very wide band of white linen or black silk swathed the neck, much care being required in its adjustment. That of Beau Brummel is said to have been twelve inches broad, and the task of "creasing down," as the operation was termed, devolved upon his faithful valet, Mortimer, of the play. The head was at first tilted back, the stiff cravat being laid across the throat and lower

PLATE XXXIX. THE EMPIRE PERIOD

A. The Empire coat, collar and stock.

B. An Empire gown (from the Ladies' Monthly Museum, London, 1806).

C. An Empire overcoat (detail from a drawing by Ingres).

D. The reticule or "ridicule" of 1806.

part of the chin; very slowly the action was reversed until several stiff creases appeared in the smooth linen; lastly, the tie was fastened, leaving the head so rigid that a turn to right or left could be essayed only with difficulty. Such a scene was "shot" but cut from the screen play with John Barrymore as Beau Brummel.

The frilled shirt had a very high collar which required a deft touch in folding it over.

Breeches or "tops" were worn with Hessian boots pulled over them.

The Pantaloons.—Full length and closely fitting the body from the waist down pantaloons were popular owing to their adoption by Beau Brummel. Tight to the leg at first, they were fastened above the ankle with buttons and worn with striped stockings and low buckled shoes. As they increased in length, they were split open over the instep and caught together by loops and buttons; still later they were held down by a strap placed under the foot, which method continued until the middle of the century.

A fob, with seals depending from it, hung below the waistcoat. Sometimes two were worn, one at either side. The overcoat was made with three or four capes reaching to just below the shoulder line. The snuff box was considered very important. Beaver hats, now grown quite tall, were the mode.

The Hair.—Wigs had gone out of style; the hair was worn short and very full at the sides of the face. Side whiskers in bushy effect were very fashionable.

WOMEN

The Empire Gown.—This fashion resulted from the revival of the classic Greek in women's clothes. For a few years the beautiful lines of this dress were untampered with, but by 1810 its length was curtailed and the sleeve was receiving the attention of the arbiters of fashion. In 1803 it was high waisted with a low-cut neck and a long skirt reaching the floor which was trained for full dress. The sleeve was merely a fanciful puff at the shoulder.

A habit shirt of "clear muslin" called a "dicky" was gathered to a neckband edged with a tiny ruff and was used to fill in the neck on walking-dresses; there was also a half-habit shirt which stopped below the collar-bone, leaving the throat bare. A pelice was a short jacket with long sleeves worn wide open in front.

Materials and Decoration.—Plain and figured muslins, and fine cambrics, manufactured in England, were extremely fashionable. Evening gowns were made of muslin, plain white being popular and gold and silver considered very elegant. Sarsenet was also in style. Gold fringe enjoyed a great vogue. Wide borders of lace finished nearly all gowns. A "curricle" was a lace overskirt reaching to the knee. Swansdown, a very popular trimming, was used to edge gowns and hats, whole muffs being fashioned of it. The last mentioned were now so enormous that arms could be buried in them to the elbows, a comfortable fashion with sleeves non-existent. India shawls were stylish. A bag or reticule, commonly called "a ridicule," was carried.

Gloves, Shoes and Hats.—Gloves, reaching to the short puffed sleeves, were held in place by armlets of pearl, gold, silver or enamel, some representing wreaths of flowers. A shorter glove, reaching to below the elbow, was also worn.

A shade known as "York Tan," was most in demand, but white and buff were used, too.

Heelless shoes like slippers, in white or blue (often mazarine blue), scarlet, green, yellow or "straw" and made of silk, velvet, and white leather were the correct mode.

Beaver hats in imitation of the men's were popular; straw bonnets fitting the head were trimmed with flowers.

The Hair.—A bunch of curls was caught on top with a row of small ones across the brow. The most popular headdress was a wreath of silver or a bandeau of flowers, with heron's feathers, a "prince's feather" or an ostrich plume occasionally topping them. Turbans of colored velvet were edged with swansdown.

The sleeve developed into a series of puffs which extended from shoulder to wrist. A long, loose undersleeve gathered to a wrist ruffle was worn when the former short shoulder puff was retained. Ruffles appeared as trimming on the skirt and about the neck; fichus so decorated were worn crossed on the bosom and tied behind. The skirt reached only to the ankles.

Tall straw hats were tied with ribbon under the chin.

In 1817, braiding was used on the bodice in imitation of a soldier's uniform. Mary Astor wore a gown so trimmed in the latter part of "Beau Brummel."

The shoes were low, with round toes.

During the Empire, jewelry was massive in form, the extremely low necks affording much area for cameos and large gems in elaborate settings. Earrings were long and heavy. Jewels were used in trimming turbans, and also to catch up the puff sleeve on evening gowns.

Parasols, heavily fringed, were carried.

PLATE XL. GEORGIAN, EMPIRE AND VICTORIAN COSTUMES

A. The monkey-tailed sack, 1770.
B. The enormous hoop skirt, 1860.
C and D. A gentleman of 1823 and a lady of 1815.
E. A man of the Empire period.

GEORGE IV, 1820 1830

Men

Trousers were strapped under the instep, those known as "peg-top" being very full about the hips and narrowing down to a tight fit at the ankles. The coat, retaining much of the same cut, was made in quiet colors such as buff, blue or gray, its collar high but not so extravagantly so as during the Empire.

A white collar, with high points lying up against the jawbone, was worn with a stock of black silk or satin wrapped about it. The shirts were very much frilled.

The Wellington boot, low-heeled, round-toed and reaching to above the ankle, was in style.

The hair was now bushy at the front with the sides brushed forward toward the eyes. Eyeglasses were suspended on black silk ribbon. Fobs were very fashionable.

High beaver hats were in style.

Women

Round, full skirts were worn over stiff petticoats. The waist, short and pointed in front, was adjusted over a corset, the shoulder seam dropping and the sleeve growing larger. Evening gowns left the shoulders bare.

The hair was parted in the center and arranged with clusters of curls about the forehead and sides of the face.

WILLIAM IV, 1830-1837

Men

Coats had velvet collars and cuffs, trousers remaining the same. Overcoats were made with long capes to the

PLATE XLI. NINETEENTH-CENTURY ACCESSORIES

A. Poke bonnet, 1845.
B. Lace shawl over hoops, 1860.
C. Back hair held in a beaded net, 1865.
D and E. Bathing girl and a watcher on the beach (drawing from a print in *Frank Leslie's,* 1859).

waist; this fashion lasted a long time.   High beaver hats were still the mode.

The Hair.—The hair was full about the face, some men using a center parting.   A new note was the mutton-chop whisker, which curved forward on the cheek; mustaches began to appear.

WOMEN

The Leg O' Mutton Sleeve.—This was a startling and extremely ugly fashion, the culmination of the ever descending armhole.   An enormous sleeve presenting a swollen, balloonlike appearance from shoulder to elbow, became skin-tight to the wrist.   The waist had grown very small, owing to the introduction of stays and lacing. The skirt, standing stiffly out from the figure, reached to just above the ankles.   A crowning touch was given this leg o' mutton ensemble by perching a wide brimmed hat, decorated profusely with flowers or feathers, over the curly top-knot with its high supporting comb.

VICTORIA, 1837-1901; THE VICTORIAN PERIOD

MEN

The Coat.—Light trousers were much worn early in the reign, the coat changing gradually to the frock and the Prince Albert for formal wear.   The skirts were rounded off in front on morning coats.   Colored waistcoats were worn.   The stock and high-pointed collar went out of fashion about 1860, when a low turned-down collar began to take their place.   During the seventies a very high choker collar was used with very short coats.   Cutaways, sack coats, Prince Alberts and frock coats con-

tinued in style throughout the century, as did the dress suit
of black broadcloth known as the "swallow-tail," with
slight alterations in its cut from time to time.

The Tuxedo.—In the early nineties a coat of black
broadcloth or other fine material, and made without tails,
was adopted by young men for "smokers." It was known
as the "tuxedo" and not considered strictly full dress.

In the eighties the "blazer," a coat made of bright colored striped flannel, was popular for summer country
wear. White duck or flannel trousers accompanied it, a
silk sash taking the place of a belt.

Headgear.—Black, white or fawn colored high hats of
silk or beaver were made with bell-shaped crowns before
1860. Their brims became tight rolled, with straight tops.
High hats of white or gray felt were in fashion until
1890. Those of silk plush made on a pasteboard frame
were considered more formal when the derby, black, brown
and gray, became popular. The height and contour of the
latter changed from year to year. Straw hats took the
form of the "sailor" in the nineties.

The Hair.—Beards became very fashionable in the
early Victorian era; side whiskers were also worn. Men
extended the center parting of their hair back to the nape
of the neck, which resulted in a fullness over the ears.
One style familiar in pictures of Lord Tennyson, permitted the locks to grow very long. The pompadour, suggesting an inverted shoe-brush, was popular in the eighties.
A middle parting, with the hair worn long and drooping
over the temples, was for a time succeeding this affected by
young men, alternating with a side parting and the hair
brushed back. The latter form continued after the other.

Footgear.—The boot known as "congress" with side

insets of elastic which did away with fastening, and low
heels, was the most popular form of foot covering for
years. For evening wear, pumps were worn; these toward
the end of the century were of patent leather. Men wore
buttoned or laced shoes from the seventies on. Russet
and various shades of tanned leather came into style during the last decade. Oxford ties of white canvas or
tanned leather replaced them in summer.

Neckwear and Jewelry.—The small necktie, purchased
made up with a long band attached to go around the collar,
was succeeded by the kind which required self-tying.
Large cravats called Ascots were made up by knotting and
crossing the two wide ends of padded satin or silk, which,
when so arranged and held by a scarf pin, completely filled
the V-opening of the vest. Four-in-hand ties replaced
them. Bow or string ties were always popular.

Gold or silver watches were carried in a lower vest
pocket; heavy chains with seal and ornamental key attached hung across the vest and were secured to a buttonhole by a bar. Fobs were also used. In the sixties gold
pencils with large jewels set in the end were fashionable.

WOMEN

Pantalettes.—At the beginning of Victoria's reign the
skirts were made so full and short that the modesty of the
time required the wearing of pantalettes. These rather resembled muslin pillowcases and were gathered to the legs
by means of elastic run through at top and bottom. Lace
frills attached to their lower edges flopped about the ankles.
By 1860 only the old-fashioned wore them.

The sleeve had taken on a round balloon shape; this
gradually straightened out, losing all fullness at the arm-

PLATE XLII. THE EIGHTEEN-SEVENTIES, -EIGHTIES
AND -NINETIES

A. 1875. The Grecian bend.

B. The bustle of the seventies (from cartoons by Grevin).

C. 1886. Bonnet, dolman and overskirt showing shawl drapery over the bustle.

D. The large sleeve and gored skirt of the nineties.

liole, which now was normal. A wide bell shape, of elbow length, became fashionable in the sixties. With it was worn an undersleeve, often of expensive lace or the finest lawn exquisitely embroidered, cut very full and gathered to a tiny wristband.

The Hoop Skirt.—Crinoline petticoats, made with many flounces and stiffened with whalebone, were used to inflate the skirts. By 1855 the hoop appeared. It was constructed in this wise: from a broad band about the waist, others depended to which huge hoops of whalebone were attached, gradually widening in circumference as they descended to the floor. A valance of lace and lawn was attached to its inside for concealment in case of tilting. The hoop skirt became *passé* in 1863, when it was replaced by flounced crinoline petticoats.

The very small-waisted bodice, running to long points at front and back, was boned and laced. Evening gowns were worn off the shoulders, their sleeves standing out in flattened puffs. With the bell sleeves, a high-necked waist, with a round collar of embroidery or lace matching the undersleeves, was used. Honiton and point lace were very fashionable.

The waist accompanying the hoop-skirted evening gown had no sleeves; it was cut very low, the front and back meeting in a narrow band slipped below the shoulder. All waists as a rule laced up the back.

The Poke Bonnet.—The poke bonnet made its entry about 1840. It was made with a wide arching brim under which roses or other flowers were placed against the hair; its crown rose to a high puff with a curtain of lace or silk hanging across the back of the neck. Wide ribbons secured this coquettish affair beneath the chin.

Caps.—White caps were worn by all matrons. These were often quite imposing, very full of frilled lace and ribbons. When ladies went to stay overnight or spend the day, a two-handled basket of wicker, opening through its center somewhat after the fashion of a lunch basket, was carried. In it reposed the fresh, frilly cap, while on their heads sat another crushed under a poke bonnet. Sometimes they were made with long tabs hanging each side of the face. Their heyday was in the forties and fifties.

The Hair.—This was parted in the middle with clusters of curls at either side—a fashion accompanying the poke bonnet. Long braids, composed of many strands and interwoven until they looked like basketwork, were wound about the ears by young girls. The hair of older women was brought over the ears and fastened in a knot at the back, from which long curls were carried forward over the shoulders. The smoothly brushed hair caught planes of light as it curved about the head. During the sixties the back hair was caught in a coarse, meshed net resembling a caul; a narrow black velvet ribbon was run through its edge and tied in a bow on the crown of the head.

Poke bonnets of a smaller size, also wide-brimmed leghorn hats, were worn. With the long riding habit which trailed from the left hip, a silk hat resembling a man's was used.

Prunella boots or congress gaiters with elastic insets on the sides were made of black cloth. The slippers of 1860 had no heels whatsoever; the boots only a small elevation. This lasted until the seventies.

The Seventies.—By 1870 the dress clung to the figure except at the back, where a bustle made its appearance. All materials, save the gauzes used on evening gowns, were heavy and opaque; yards and yards were piled in draperies over the bustle, descending thence in a train. Ruffles, flounces, bands, borders—all of them fringed—were placed in every conceivable position on the front of the skirt. The basque, tight fitting and boned, was high necked, the trimming on the elbow sleeves duplicating that in the skirt. On evening gowns the neck was cut higher at the back. Ruffles, ruches and the like trimmed it.

The Chignon or Waterfall.—The hair was carried high on the back of the head, then allowed to descend in a cascade of ringlets.

A bonnet, tilting forward over the forehead, was placed in front of the chignon. With this was affected the Grecian bend, *i.e.*, the body was bent forward from the waist so that the lady with her bustle advanced somewhat like a camel.

High heels were worn. Shoes of bronze leather fastened up the front by many little buttoned straps were very stylish.

The Eighties.—The bustle was still worn but by 1890 it had gone out completely. The skirt was cut round, being trained only for night. The hour-glass figure was the fashion. The basque fitted like a glove over a high corset, closely boned and well laced. Not a. wrinkle was permitted anywhere; sleeves exactly fitted the armhole. The waist was cut in sections; the material of which it was to be made and a piece of heavy lining of silk or muslin, the two exactly matching in form, were then basted together. When all the corresponding parts were so arranged, the whole cut-out puzzle was carefully joined and fitted until no pucker remained. Every seam and dart was stiffened with whalebone, the latter being covered with

Squirrel lined "circulars" of black silk, ankle length, were very popular in the early eighties. Dolmans of brocaded velvet trimmed with chenille fringe, had fitted backs reaching to just below the waist, long hanging fronts, and loose pieces covering the arms. The back was pulled in by a ribbon attached at the waistline underneath and tied in front.

The chignon was discarded, the hair being curled on top of the head; across the forehead a bang or "fringe" was worn. Some women arranged their tresses in a knot at the nape of the neck, as worn by Lily Langtry, the most famous beauty of the time. Either way, the ears showed.

Small bonnets, made of fine material and with care, were worn well back on the head and tied with strings under the ear. Hats of felt had tall crowns and close-rolled brims; leghorns, flower trimmed, were also worn.

The Nineties.—The skirt was cut in gores, lined, and stiffened around the bottom with crinoline, starched petticoats helping to distend it. The waist fitted the corseted figure and the sleeves, which had begun to show a slight fullness at the shoulder in the last three years of the eighties, were gradually enlarged, taking on various forms which included a revival of the leg o' mutton of 1830, with the important difference that it was attached to a normal armhole. These sleeves were lined with crinoline and their set was important; women fussed side by side in street cars, each endeavoring to place her own in front of her neighbor's lest they be crushed. The hats were perky, turned up at the back, and much trimmed. Long cape coats, also long tight-fitting ones, were worn. Sealskin (real, not muskrat) was the mode for fur coats. Tailored suits of serge and various other cloths were introduced, all with large-topped sleeves. High shoes, both buttoned and laced, were worn, oxford ties taking their place in summer.

The Shirt Waist.—The craze for this had its outset in 1893, in time spreading even to the men. It was at first strictly tailored of colored or white linen, China silk, or percale with a stiff high collar and laundered cuffs. The four-in-hand tie, cuff buttons and belt which accompanied it became objects of much attention. Belts were mostly of leather with fancy buckles. Some women preferred tiny silk girdles laced in front or ribbons finished with bows.

Later the tailored look disappeared and the fashion of elaborately trimmed, separate waists made of silks, satin, velvets, foulards, lace, etc., lasted for a long while. With the addition of several well made skirts, usually black, say one of cloth, one of satin, and another of some light crêpey material, a woman was provided with an extensive wardrobe.

Up to this time a woman's skin, excepting that of her face, had always been invisible on the street due to the opaque materials in use. Toward the end of the century, however, English eyelet embroidery became fashionable and shirt waists were made of it. This was considered as scandalous as it was unprecedented—that the neck and arms of woman, her very flesh itself, should be exposed through the tiny openings in the goods! It also became a staple for joke-makers. Much is said against the modern flapper, but the so-called *fin de siècle* girl gave her Victorian mother many a jolt.

The "shirtwaist man," who arrived soon after, was regarded with horror by many females. His retort was that if he could sit in an open car and gaze upon the skin of woman, why then should not he be coatless and comfortable in a starched, immaculate shirt that was quite opaque?

Gauzes and chiffons were used in evening gowns; the necks cut round and low, the sleeves mere puffs hanging below the shoulder. In the wake of the eyelet embroidery followed a stream of sheer materials, chiffons, voiles, and finally georgette becoming the mode for street use; lace yokes were put in dresses.

With the end of the century a train was attached to a skirt that fitted smoothly over the hips and flared below the knees. Gowns and shirt waists, made with full elbow-length sleeves, were fastened up the back; this was the age when women had to be hooked up. Hats were large and much befeathered. Muffs and long boas reaching to the knees were in style; the latter made of ostrich or coque feathers for summer.

Houses up to this time had depended largely on heating methods not so effective as those of to-day, and what was known as "heavy underwear" was considered necessary for the winter months. These heavy silk, all wool, or wool and cotton mixed, garments, long sleeved and ankle length, were systematically changed to, almost as a rite, at the first nip of frost.

Jewelry.—Victorian jewelry in the sixties comprised sets of pin, earrings, bracelets and necklaces. Very large brooches and wide bracelets were much worn. Watches enclosed in gold cases were, during the time mentioned, attached to long gold chains often studded with gems and fastened to a matching pin placed at the collar opening. In the nineties, the watch, now open faced, was tucked inside the bosom of the gown between its hooks, while a shower of charms, pendant to tiny chains, hung from it.

Earrings became very long in the seventies; in the eighties, solitaires (single diamonds) were in the ears of every woman who could afford them, or rhinestones and paste imitations substituted. The fashion, except for older women, went out in the nineties; all earrings had been worn like rivets through a hole in the lobe of the ear, but now the younger set revolted, considering it a relic of barbarism.

Bangles, chains and jeweled snake bracelets superseded the round, heavily chased ones of gold.

Lockets were in style during the entire Victorian period, in fact, they endured until displaced by the La Vallière, which made its appearance early in the present century. In 1895 a variety of locket known as the "Trilby heart," made of gold or silver, hung on a long chain of the same metal about the neck of every woman.

"Chatelaine" bags of black velvet suspended from the waist by a silver chain and hook, also beaded bags, knitted purses and "portemonnaies" of the Victorian age were followed by the leather pocketbook with many small receptacles and one closed for money, the covering flap fastened on the side by a metal catch. This, in the eighties and nineties, was carried in the muff, pocket (the wide seams in the skirt boasted pockets), or openly in the hand. Alligator bags, fashioned like miniature traveling luggage, were used during the same period.

Veils.—Face veils reaching to the nose were suspended from the brim of the tilted hat in the seventies. In the nineties a craze for veils swept over the world of women, driving the eye-doctors to exasperation, for the chenille

PLATE XLIV. HEADDRESSING, NINETEENTH AND TWENTIETH
CENTURIES

A. The chignon or waterfall, 1872.
B. The chignon or waterfall, 1874.
C. Bang and Langtry knot of the eighties.
D. The curled bang of the nineties.
E. The picture hat of 1830.
F. The bonnet of 1883.
G. Pompadour and pointed collar, 1903.
H. The Merry Widow hat, 1908.
I. The pompadour and ribbon collar ending in a bow at the back,
1898.

dot reigned supreme. This, in varying sizes, was spread over the whole surface of the veil either separately or symmetrically clustered, necessitating great care in the pinning on in order to achieve a becoming, and not disfiguring, arrangement.

Long chiffon veils in various colors were pinned around the hat, thrown up off the face and allowed to fly backward in the breeze. Frenchwomen had a strong penchant for those of white lace, which always had an especial allure. "Complexion veils" were of the finest white or gray gauze with an overlay pattern in the sheerest black thread.

Young girls of the nineties cast off the high, ugly corset and wore a girdle about five inches wide, which merely laced the figure about the waist. Their Victorian mothers were, of course, aghast. The flapper of the Mauve Decade had fired the first shot. Other women of a common sense and rather mannish style, a type of new woman the world was then viewing for the first time, took to wearing Ferris waists; these were made without bones and gave them a dowdy, shapeless look.

CHAPTER XXIV

THE TWENTIETH CENTURY

HE gown was now worn over a "straight front" corset, the cut of the latter being much lower in front than heretofore, and with no inward curve at the waistline. Boning was no longer used in waists and lining disappeared. But the back fastening was still the vogue.

The waist was made to blouse out over the waistline by cutting the front section much too long and wide; tiny tucks were then placed at each side, extending vertically some five inches from the neck line until a smooth fit was created across the bosom; the fullness was gathered in a dipping curve and raised to the waistline—an effect which can be seen in any picture of the Gibson girl of that time. The skirt spread out about the feet, ending in a train which was held up in the street, and supported while dancing by running the hand through a ribbon loop. High collars running up in points behind the ears were still worn on street dresses. For evening, the tiny sleeve was slipped down and straps about an inch wide and variously ornamented, were placed over the shoulders to support the gown.

Laced shoes with pointed toes and heels of various heights were for street wear, high French-heeled slippers for dancing.

Very long ostrich feather boas and small neck ruffs of

feathers, pleated chiffon, ribbon and the like were common and were superseded by stoles twelve inches in width and made of coque feathers, marabou or fur. Muffs were large. Neckpieces of fox and other small animals came into style.

The Merry Widow Hat.—In 1908 a wide-brimmed, befeathered hat, which stood high on the pompadour, took its name from the most popular light opera of the day. A craze for this hat developed and ostrich plumes became greatly in demand; the variety known as "willow," drooping over the crowns, was soon followed by "glycerined" and novelty feathers, many resembling those in feather dusters.

The Peach Basket Hat.—Well named, for its advent, in 1909, suddenly sent the hair of women into a concealment from which to this day, whenever a hat is on the head, it has not emerged. It had a huge crown whose brim was merely a continuation; flowers flattened against it and ruchings applied in designs formed the trimming. Lace and fine pleated ruffles sometimes were used in lieu of the brim. Hats eventually regained their brims, but the crown, perhaps largely due to motoring, still hides the hair. With the innovation of this tight-fitting crown, hat pins, which had flourished for years and had become very ornate, expensive, dangerous—and, of course, food for the comic papers because of their great length—went into limbo.

The Hobble Skirt.—The fullness of the skirt when it lost its train was for a short time, in the summer of 1910, drawn in about the feet by an elastic band. This proved a fleet whim of fashion and by no means universal, due not only to the accidents resulting from its wear, but largely to its ugliness and inconvenience. It completely changed the silhouette, however, for the skirt became straight and sheathlike, measuring less than a yard around its lower edge.

Women walked with difficulty and boarding a street car was impossible without hoisting the gown to the knees. The low steps on cars of the Broadway line in New York City were designed just for that—to help the ladies. Despite the absurdity of this fashion, a desperate hue and cry was raised when French mannequins appeared at Longchamps in skirts slashed open to the knee; yet this radical suggestion led to a way out when fanlike pleatings were inserted in the opening—and so, women were enabled to walk once more.

The Rainy Day Skirt.—Meanwhile, a club was formed in New York City by women who, disgusted with the long and trailing unsanitary skirts, pledged themselves to wear short (that is to say, short for those still prudish days) round skirts on wet days. One called the "trotteur" was also launched by the French modistes for shopping and walking. But there is no doubt that the sensible women, the "rainy Daisies" early in this century, who ran the gantlet of ridicule, were unwittingly responsible for today's abbreviated skirts.

Dresses were almost Empire in line before the World War, with a high waistline, long, wrinkled sleeves and slim, clinging skirts fashioned of cêpe de Chine, soft satins and georgettes. During the duration of hostilities, dresses of all kinds became short, the shoe top being decreed for a long time the right length. Footwear grew conveniently accommodating, however, and rose to surprising heights, boasting many buttons. So did the spat, of gray, fawn or black, worn above low shoes in winter.

The Blouse.—The shirt waist, or blouse, as it became

known, was only used as an adjunct to the suit. Voile, georgette, lace, satin and crêpe de Chine, with lace frills, insertions, and even beading, were used in its making. It was tucked inside of the belt, subjecting the figure to a most trying outline on removal of the coat.

The Kimona Sleeve.—The introduction of the middy blouse, also the fashion of the tunic and the kimona sleeve, gradually changed this and eliminated the hooked-up-the-back frock, also the one with intricate shoulder and side fastenings. Fashion reverted to the tunic of the ancients; the uncorseted woman thrust her head through a neck opening, her arms into kimona sleeves—and was comfortable. Unfortunately, only too often she looked it!

Jewelry.—The La Vallière, an arrangement of jewels forming a pendant, hung on a gold or silver chain about the neck until displaced by the fad for necklaces of graduated and usually imitation pearls. In varying lengths, that known as the "opera" reached to the bosom. Strings of colored beads were to be had in endless variety. The present century differs from its forerunners in its predilection for synthetic stones, largely due to the influence of French *nouveau art* jewelry. Platinum superseded gold as settings for diamonds, these stones attaining a much greater value than ever before. One innovation was the use of platinum for wedding rings. Many women went to the extreme of having theirs of gold, telltale evidence of marriages made at dates preceding the fashion, covered with platinum. In the last year, however, owing to the cheap imitations of platinum, there has been a return to gold for settings.

Earrings, due to the fact that now they were designed with screw backs, making unnecessary the piercing of ears, achieved a popular revival. In all lengths and of infinite variety they have appeared, and are invariably becoming.

The fad for bar pins reached its height with the tunic dress, which was anchored by placing one across the bosom. Cameos have also had a vogue.

Bracelets never actually go out of fashion; they merely vary. The present craze known as "the slave," threatens to become so common that its doom is merely a question of time. The wrist watch served as a bracelet for a long while, the merely useful variety being attached to a strap of black silk or leather. More ornate ones were of platinum studded with diamonds. Many jingling bracelets worn with the short-sleeved gown or on the sleeveless arm, have pushed the wrist watch to the wall. Narrow flexible bands set with diamonds and sapphires, the latter usually synthetic, have been worn for several years. The present tendency is a reversion to the broad bands of flexible gold of mid-Victorian days.

Marquise rings set with diamonds were very fashionable early in the century, knuckle to knuckle being the prescribed length. Then came a procession of dinner rings large and decorative, rings to match the necklace, rings to match the gown in color, and, lastly, two large matching stones to adorn the fingers. Luckily the fashion does not involve the nose!

Low shoes have created a demand for handsome buckles; this winter the high heel of the slipper is jewel studded.

The "choker" is at present the most popular form of necklace. The stores are loaded with "junk" and women buy and buy.

Veils.—These for many, many years were thought an

indispensable part of a woman's attire; the chiffon veil,
variously colored, was draped on all hats early in the century and used for motoring; white lace veils of French
make were festooned across the *chapeau* or worn tight to
the face. Women actually felt undressed if they sallied
forth without a veil; and much time was spent posing
before a counter mirror while selecting one most calcu-
lated to soften the features or hide wrinkles. The fashion
died out about the time of the Great War and its passing
was attributable not only to the ever increasing popularity
of the bob but also to the use of hair nets.

The Handbag.—This, as we know, arrived with the
present century. Not very large at first, it had a metal
top and a chain to carry it by, and a pouch of leather, velvet or beaded material. Small mesh bags of gunmetal,
also of silver, were in style. By 1910, with pockets gone
from dresses, the handbag had become indispensable.
Mesh bags of gold and silver, together with the beaded
bag, are always the dressiest. The useful variety of
leather has undergone many changes in shape and size.
A few years ago the "under-arm" bag superseded for a
time the hanging form in popularity; it was merely an
enormous wallet or envelope purse. The handbags of the
present year have attained the greatest size ever known in
the history of this accessory, so dear to every woman.

After the War the low shoe attained such a vogue that
the high variety disappeared almost entirely. Only silk
stockings now were used, even on the coldest days, and
the doctors, scolding, spoke of pneumonia. Then some
frozen flapper took to wearing woolen hose. Sensible,
but suggestive of the peasant, these stockings were all

right in their proper place—for sports and with sport clothes. Unfortunately, they were too often worn with frocks and coats intended for dress occasions. The advent of the flesh-colored, lining stocking of fine wool, over which the sheerest silk hose can be drawn without any appreciable increase in the size of the ankle, has been adopted by many women for use during frigid weather.

Meditating on the undergarments of a flapper, one wonders why the lingerie departments in our big stores do not fail. The little specialty shops tucked in between the theatres along Broadway, dotting the side streets and even asserting themselves impertinently on Fifth Avenue, display in the limited space of their windows quantities of lacy, airy trifles which now are considered all that the modern girl requires as underwear. Through the gauze stockings hanging in the foreground can be seen other equally sheer and crushable garments. One windowful would dress many girls.

Low shoes seem to have run the gamut of all possible shapes, and of variety in the strappings, with the craze still unabated. At present the working in of different colored leathers seems to be occupying the maker's attention.

The flapper who slopped about with unfastened goloshes because it "made her feel more blah," has succeeded in appropriating the really fashionable to herself, and herself alone; older women cannot share in it without appearing ridiculous. Everywhere we see girls of twenty and older, whose skirts do not reach the knees. This is an extreme which older women of society, supposed to be style leaders, have not yet dared to follow. But the most radical through all the ages has ever been the height of fashion.

Older women with thinning hair look pathetic with it bobbed, and yet some misguided ones have parted with their locks in order to achieve the fashionable silhouette. Bobbed hair has survived so long mainly because, if it is allowed to start growing, its wearer finds short, scraggly locks extremely difficult of arrangement in the daytime; at night every girl is provided with a switch of her own or some one else's hair with which to bind the head. The boyish bob, however, seems to have sounded the knell for this coiffure—nought remains but a close shave!

Women, realizing that lack of corsets was enlarging waist and hip, flew in a panic to the rubber kind intended for reduction; these, while on, undoubtedly made the figure trimmer. Step-ins or wrap-arounds, either all elastic or in combination with boned brocade, the present idea in correct corseting, seem to offer a more healthful solution of the problem.

The Brassière.—The old-fashioned lace-trimmed and beribboned, white muslin corset cover that took to boning its darts, was superseded by the brassière, a contrivance which, in the course of its development, made possible the fashion known as the "boyish form"; this succeeded in pressing down the figure until a flat chest, neither beautiful nor healthful, resulted.

The Fur Coat.—Gone are the days of "winter flannels," but the flapper is not responsible; her mother shed them when georgette crêpe became fashionable and the fur coat began its reign. Of course, "sealskin sacques," real mink and ermine capes, chinchilla and Russian sable wraps, had been in the wardrobe of the wealthy in the last century. But in the twentieth, heavy underwear was betrayed by the transparency of the new materials and accordingly discarded for Milanese silk or lacy, crêpey confections; women generally found that, while gowns of georgette and other unlined, thin materials were comfortable in a steam-heated room, fur was necessary for outdoor, winter wear. So motorists protected themselves with raccoon, while pony skin and Persian lamb led off for street wear, to be followed by every variety of fur from Russian sable to rabbit, the choice depending on the pocketbook.

For stage wear, only the softest and most crushable furs, such as chinchilla and ermine, or clever imitations in rabbit, which admit of wrapping close about the form, are advisable; ordinary fur is prone to give the figure a bulky shapelessness.

So great has been the demand for skins this winter that women have even worn what looks strangely like the coat of the placid cow. Some day they may cover themselves with fish-scales, but still will cry lustily with Lady Teazle, "Lud, Sir Peter, would you have me be out of the fashion?"

CHAPTER XXV

PEASANTS

HE national peasant costume is in many countries gradually falling into disuse, and ugly imitations of the so-called European garb are being substituted. The movies are largely responsible; they bring to far-away corners of the earth pictures of attractive stars, and fans of both sexes discard their own picturesque peasant attire and try to emulate in dress Adolphe and Pola. So true is this that in Italy alone, one must travel to Sardinia in order to find a distinctive costume. In fact, it has become the custom in all European countries to wear the ancient national and local peasant dress only for festivals.

Climate and local products always have had much to do with the materials used. Woolen cloth, for ages a staple product in most parts of Europe, was generally used in the colder portions; linen and silk, dyed in brilliant colors, were found more suitable for the south. Silk was manufactured in Italy and Spain at an early date; the cheaper grades were procured by the well-to-do peasants for festivals. From the days of the Gauls, dyeing was a much practiced art among the peasants; ancient manuscripts show us bright greens, blues, reds, etc. For holidays, the costumes of all countries are colorful. Tillers of the soil, however, of course found brown, gray and black more suitable; and such hues, enlivened with blue, maroon, green and scarlet, are used in the dress of stage peasants. In

PLATE XLV. SPANISH AND ITALIAN PEASANTS

A and B. A Spanish peasant and a toreador.
C. Spanish girl in mantilla and shawl.
D and E. Neapolitans.
F and G. A Roman girl and a peasant from the Campagna.

addition caps, aprons, boots and laced jerkins, all of leather, are worn by the men. For women, the costume with slight variations consists of a white cap of the shape known as "mob," a laced front bodice of cloth or velvet worn over a white shirt with puffed elbow sleeves and a round ruffled neckband, a cloth skirt with stripes of velvet or fancifully colored braid running horizontally above the hem, white stockings and low buckled shoes, frequently tongued. This ensemble has been the chief standby of costumers for all comic opera or musical comedy peasantry, no matter what the country or time, since stage dressing has been given any thought. In most details, it belongs rightfully to Switzerland and Hungary.

In dressing peasants for any date prior to the Great War, both the style typical of the nation and coloring selected to harmonize with the mood of the scene, should be considered. White caps and kerchiefs are wrong notes in scenes of sordid tragedy. These, with aprons, should be in dull colors.

The most brilliant of peasant costumes may, for amateur productions, be achieved by investing in dull shades of cheap material from which shawls, skirts, aprons, handkerchiefs and waistcoats can be cut. From bright colored muslins, make narrow bands in various widths. Stitch five or six different colored rows of these horizontally about the bottoms of skirts and aprons, running stripes of cheap tinsel braid between. Buy several yards of gay cretonne in different patterns; cut out the flowers, butterflies, birds and foliage and appliqué to the fringed shawls, aprons, kerchiefs and the like. If tastefully done an effective imitation of hand embroidery is given the audience.

Cloth hoods having capes attached were worn with or

PLATE XLVI. FRENCH AND GERMAN PEASANTS

A and B. French peasants of the nineteenth century.
C and D. The costumes of Brittany.
E, F and G. A German fishwife, a Tyrolean and flower **girl**.
H. A German peasant of the Middle Ages.

without caps or hats placed over them all through the Middle Ages. Tunics varied in length, but were never trained. Garterings of leather and straw fastened cloth to the legs of the peasants long after well fitting tights were common among the rich. Until a few years ago, rustics of England wore the smock frock, often of russet brown or gray with collar and wrist bands worked in color, knee breeches, rough cloth strapped to the leg between knee and ankle, and hobnailed shoes.

From Anglo-Saxon days, the wimple of white cloth furnished head covering for all peasant women until, with chin and forehead bands added, a stiffer style developed. The hair for centuries remained covered by starched linen, whether in the form of wimple, gorget, turban and chinband, chin clout or mob cap. Aprons, offering space for effective decoration, have been common in all countries. Bone lace and embroidery, products of arts plied by the peasants for centuries, have naturally adorned their own garments.

Circular mantles and capes were the wraps of the Middle Ages. Matting raincoats have been used in many countries, including such widely separated localities as China and Japan, Hungary and Portugal. Turbans bound the heads of East Indian peasants, while the rest of the costume, for which cotton fabrics were used, was largely negligible. In Egypt and the Holy Land linen, easier to procure than cotton, was used.

In Italy, as well as France, white caps abounded in an infinite variety, every section boasting a distinctive style. The peasant women of Milan, for centuries after all Spanish authority was removed, persisted in the use of a black mantilla of cheap lace or cloth.

PLATE XLVII. DUTCH, SWISS AND SCANDINAVIAN PEASANTS

A, B, C and D. Three Hollanders and a Swiss girl.
E and F. Swedish peasants.
G. Danish woman of the Middle Ages.
H. Northern Norwegians and Laplanders.

In Spain, also in Italy, sandals of straw shared popularity with those of leather. In Seville the usual garb is of black cloth with a black lace mantilla draped over a high comb. When leisurely promenading about the bandstands, both peasants and women of the middle class carry small fans. Young girls have adopted the "wave." Bull fights call out the gayest shawls and most beautiful of mantillas, the former being draped over the balcony railing. The bull fighters and their attendants make a kaleidoscope of colors. The long hair of the former is fastened in a knot at the back of the head; a very long sash is wound many times round the body, serving as an improvised corset. In "Blood and Sand" the winding of Otis Skinner's sash by his attendant afforded an entertaining scene. Ball trimming is much used on all parts of the costume—hat, bolero, knee pants, sash ends and garters being so decorated. The modern peasant is noticeable only because of his hat, a black affair, round of crown and brim, and a sash, often of red, about his waist.

Lace, bandings of bright braid and many buttons, appeared on the costume of French peasants, especially those of Brittany. The smock superseded the more colorful attire. Long cloth capes were much used by men; even schoolboys playing on the streets of Paris wore them.

The clothes of the Russians, Hungarians and Bulgarians have many points in common; the high wrinkled leather boot, round fur caps often with square crowns, and long coats flaring at the knee. The Russian blouse, belted and worn over loose trousers tucked into the high boot, is the typical male costume.

The Turks are fast discarding the national costume.

PLATE XLVIII. PEASANTS OF EASTERN EUROPE

A and D. Russian peasants.
B and C. A Russian Cossack and a gypsy girl.
E and H. Roumanian and Hungarian girls.
F and G. A Bulgarian and a Pole.

Trousers and veils are disappearing, and bobbed hair is quite openly flaunted—largely Gloria's fault!

The high black hat, shaped like that of Mother Goose, is resurrected by the Welsh for festivals. The Irishman's "stovepipe" drooped about the brim, its band a convenient place to hold his clay pipe; a tail coat, knee pants, striped stockings and a shillalah completed the costume. Barefooted women wore small shawls crossed on the bosom and tied at the back; their petticoats often were of red.

The male costume of Holland was chiefly remarkable for enormous trousers, direct descendants of the Flemish "slops" of Shakespeare's day. A double-breasted vest worn over a full-sleeved shirt shared popularity with a short jacket; buttons were used as decoration. A tasselled cap resembling a Victorian nightcap was much worn, also a round cap of fur. The women's caps were extremely fascinating, being of lace wired out in curving wings each side of the face. A headdress of gold wire, balls and discs can still be encountered in out-of-the-way places.

The most picturesque peasant of the New World is the Mexican in his high peaked hat with wide rolled brim, his Spanish bolero, sash, and colored handkerchief knotted about his head. A mantle or blanket is draped like a toga about the body. This frequently serves as his bed, to which he retires at any hour of the day or night, with an alley for a bedroom. The large hat is still worn, even if the costume consists only of trousers and shirt of modern cut and a blanket. The woman wears any variety of skirt and blouse, but over it she places the *rebozo*, which is usually of dark blue or black cloth and about two yards in

PLATE XLIX. OTHER PEASANT COSTUMES

A. A Welsh woman of the nineteenth century.
B, C and D. An Irish couple and an ancient Egyptian workman.
E. An Arab woman wearing the boor'cko'.
F and G. A Chinese servant and a laborer.

length. This covers her head and shoulders and one end is flung across the chest and over the left shoulder, completely covering whatever she carries, whether it be baby or market basket.

CHAPTER XXVI

SUGGESTIONS FOR CUTTING PATTERNS

OR a Houppelande.—Take a full-length dressing gown for a model and rip it apart. Cut the back long enough to drag on the floor and slightly gore the side seams on both front and back sections from waist down. The sleeve must be a long, hanging one. To get this effect cut it below the elbow in kimona fashion, making it long enough at the back to reach the floor. Extend on side of inner seam until the sleeve hangs about nine inches below the fingertips. This excess material is here turned back over the forearm, exposing a brilliant lining. The edges can be foliated or trimmed with fur. A high standing collar should rise up over the chin, then turn back for half an inch showing a lining to match that of the sleeves. Button down the front from throat to knees.

A Tunic.—Take material wide enough to reach across from shoulder to shoulder and well down over the arm. If a full-length tunic is desired, have the material more than twice the length of the body from neck to heel. The extra inches are to allow for drawing up through a girdle. Make an extra allowance for a hem. Cut out a neck opening in center of material large enough to permit the head to pass through. Sew up the sides to halfway between armpit and waistline. The opening should insure an ample armhole. Cut knee length for men (allow for hem'). For the Anglo-Saxon and Norman tunic, cut the neck opening down in a V five inches long and face it.

For Anglo-Saxon and Norman shirts, use pieced material as the armhole should extend to the waistline and the sleeve must be long enough to lay in wrinkles on the arm from elbow to wrist.

Trim the tunic according to period. For a Grecian tunic, consult Chapter IX and note that the two pieces of goods, if of crêpe de Chine or cheesecloth, must be six feet square to allow for shrinkage in width when the creased look appears.

For a Cote-Hardie.—Take a modern man's shirt. Cut off the neckband and cut out a square neck in front, five inches deep at center (a circular neck line is sometimes used). Extend back and two front sections to reach well over hip line; take in sides to shape the waistline. Stitch fronts to back portions from armpit to waist. Do not join below waistline. Open sleeve, cut off starched cuff and piece with soft material to extend well down over hand. Take sleeve in to fit securely from elbow to wrist. Button sleeve together from elbow to wrist. The neck opening is filled in by a lawn shirt gathered to a ruffled band.

The lappet, which is a band of material of contrasting color, is placed about the arm above the elbow and cut with a long streamer depending.

For a Doublet.—Leave the neckband on the shirt. Fit the sleeves and take in the side seams to the waistline. Gather the fullness to a belt which must dip a bit at the front. Then cut off the original shirt tails front and back and sew a series of square tabs below the belt, for the Elizabethan period. Place padded epaulets around the

PLATE L. DIAGRAMS FOR CUTTING

A. Shirt of a modern man with dotted lines showing how to convert it into the pattern of a cote-hardie.

B. The same with dotted lines showing alterations and additions necessary for a doublet, ruff, epaulet and hanging sleeve.

C. A tunic. Handle the goods as directed in Chapter XXVI to secure the shape suggested by dotted lines.

D. A surcoat. Follow directions in Chapter XXVI.

E. A hood. Cut double and follow directions in Chapter XV.

armhole. These and the entire doublet may be slashed and puffings of another color allowed to show through. A hanging sleeve can be suspended from the armhole over the tight-fitting under one. This should be left open down the front of the arm, and lined with imitation ermine or brilliant color. It may be caught together at intervals by jewels. To the neckband should be attached the ruff. For the Stuart period, cut the doublet with a much higher waistline and attach the tabs, which should be made much larger and fewer in number, to the doublet by means of points (*i.e.,* tagged ribbons).

For Mantles.—Use very wide material and piece the goods to form a semicircle. Lay the center of the straight side across the back of the neck and bring the rest of the material forward over each shoulder. Fasten two large fancy buttons or pins near the straight edges at each side of the chest. Attach a piece of heavy cord or a chain to the material immediately behind each button. The mantle may be cut any length desired, and its edges bordered with fur. A contrasting lining is effective.

For a Hood.—Cut two pieces of material each one yard long as in Diagram E, Plate L. On one of them cut out the material inside the dotted line, leaving an opening about seven inches long by six wide. Bind the edges. The lower end of material should be scalloped or foliated, or all edges may be bordered with fur. Stitch the front and back together. The head is inserted through the shoulder opening. The hood may be made with a much longer liripipe, and its shoulder cape may be knee length, in which case the sides are left open to the armpit. For a jester, use the hood knee length and cut the lower edge in deep points, to which attach bells.

PLATE LI. THE BODICE GOWN AS A FOUNDATION FOR VARIOUS
COSTUMES

See pages 274-275

Shoes.—A pair of felt "comfy" slippers can be cut down and covered with velvet. If the Tudor shoe is desired, make broad toes with four slashes filled with white or colored material. For the long pointed shoes, carry the velvet out several inches beyond the foot, tapering to a point and stuffing with cotton batting. This will give a medieval effect.

For the Elizabethan, Stuart, Jacobean and Georgian periods, pumps with Cuban heels are needed. To these can be attached rosettes, buckles, upstanding tongues and colored heels as desired.

Tights should be rented from a costumer.

Trunks can be made by covering a pair of bathing trunks with a bright material cut full enough to gather about the waistline and each leg. Over this loop vertical bands of another material of a darker color extending from the waistline to the lower edge of trunks.

Coats.—For the various coats of the seventeenth and eighteenth centuries, a discarded dress coat or a cutaway can be ripped apart and used as a pattern. The sections should be lengthened for the end of the seventeenth century, and pleats can be inserted on the hips for the early years of the eighteenth. The tails should be widened and stiffened with crinoline for George II, the fronts cut away for George III, and so on. See Plate XXXIV. If silk and velvet are not possible, cheap fabrics such as rayon, sateen, or even cretonne, if used with judgment, may be employed. Modern vests may be made any length for a waistcoat pattern. Cretonne may be used. Decoration for both coats and waistcoats is lace appliqué, braid and buttons, according to date.

To Make a Gown of the Middle Ages.—Use the pattern of a modern bodice-top gown, in the desired size. The back gores of the skirt may be extended to form a train and the entire hem at all points must touch the floor. Gather this skirt on about the hips. The most graceful accompanying sleeve is tight fitting to within two inches of the elbow, hanging thence in a wide flare to the floor. Observe Figure A, Plate LI, which will serve as a model for the tenth, eleventh and twelfth centuries in France, Italy and Spain and for the age of draperies in England. On the inside seam of the sleeve cut the material off six inches below the bend in the arm, which will permit turning it back against the upper arm. A lining of brilliant contrasting color is effective. This sleeve may be seen on Figure B, Plate LI, which pictures a gown with bodice top and full trailing skirt used by Jane Cowl as Melisande. Made of long trailing chiffon this sleeve is most attractive. This material or georgette may also be used for the gown and veil, the bodice being fashioned without darts. When made in orchid, delicate green or blue, etc., over a slip of a deeper shade or contrasting color, this is a very charming· model for plays of a poetic character dealing with the· Ancient Britons or Italian, Spanish and English people of the Middle Ages. A tight-fitting undersleeve of another color may show from elbow to wrist finishing in a point over the back of the· hand. Sarah Bernhardt affected these to her knuckles. Buttons running down the outside of this sleeve may be utilized to secure a snug fit about the· wrist and hand. Another style loops the full gored skirt up in front by pulling it through a cord girdle placed low about the hips. This is the kirtle gown accompanied by the gorget which is pictured on Figure C, Plate LI. Under it a skirt of another color must reach

the floor. One or both may receive border decoration.
The long tight sleeve should have puffs of another color
inserted at the shoulder and elbow; small puffs may also
extend up the outer seam from wrist to shoulder. For
the early sixteenth century, slashing may be used on
epaulets placed about the armhole. The virago sleeve
(see sixteenth century, p. 146), may be used with this
gown.

With the hennin and steeple headdress, the bodice
should be cut very low around the shoulders and fastened
by lapping one front across the other at a high waistline.
(See Figure F, Plate XVIII.) The trained skirt with the
sleeves sweeps the floor.

For a simarre, fit the bodice to well down on the hips.
Attach a skirt, which must be straight and clinging in
front and trained at the back. Cover the joint round the
hips by a girdle, which may pass twice about the body
before being knotted low in front. An elbow sleeve that
reaches the floor is always the prettiest. Observe Figures
F and G, Plate LI, which may be selected as models for
Anglo-Saxon and Norman gowns. The tunic pattern
may be used (see Figure C, Plate L), the material chosen
being the width of the hips.

Heart-Shaped and Horn.—With the horned and heart-
shaped headdresses, use the cote-hardie and a trained
skirt. The bodice pattern, well fitted, may serve as a pattern for the cote-hardie, which should be made in imitation of Figure I, Plate XIV. By using a fitted bodice
top and full round skirt, a very pretty Spanish costume
may be evolved. See Figure E, Plate LI.

For the tightly laced bodices and basques of the
eighteenth and nineteenth centuries, a well corseted figure

is a first necessity. For a pattern let some attic yield up a fitted basque of the eighties. Ripped up, it will be in eight pieces. These must be carefully pinned together until a perfect unwrinkled surface is achieved. The slits in the front sections are taken in to form darts under the bust. The basque can be used on the Watteau gown and on all gowns from 1830 to 1895. Sleeves and the neck line must be cut to follow the changing mode.

INDEX

(2)